SOMETIMES WE WEAR PAJAMAS TO CHURCH

Jen Talley
with Mike Talley

NEW HARBOR PRESS

RAPID CITY, SD

Copyright © 2023 by Jen Talley

All rights reserved. No part of this publication may be reproduced, distributed or transmitted in any form or by any means, including photocopying, recording, or other electronic or mechanical methods, without the prior written permission of the publisher, except in the case of brief quotations embodied in critical reviews and certain other noncommercial uses permitted by copyright law. For permission requests, write to the publisher, addressed "Attention: Permissions Coordinator," at the address below.

Talley/New HarborPress
1601 Mt. Rushmore Rd, Ste 3288
Rapid City, SD 57701
www.newharborpress.com

Ordering Information:
Quantity sales. Special discounts are available on quantity purchases by corporations, associations, and others. For details, contact the "Special Sales Department" at the address above.

Book cover designed by Catherine Garrett

Sometimes We Wear Pajamas to Church/Jen Talley. -- 1st ed.
ISBN 978-1-63357-272-0

Contents

Opening Words 1

The Story Behind the Title 3

Sometimes It Comes Down to Relationship 9

Sometimes We Parent from Our Pain—Mike Talley ...27

Sometimes We Correct 39

Sometimes We Parent Differently................................47

Sometimes We Are Little 59

Sometimes We Are Big 69

Sometimes We Have Hormones 79

Sometimes We Fall in Love... 89

Sometimes We Need to Say Sorry...............................105

Sometimes We Serve—Mike Talley 115

Final Thoughts...125

Recommended Readings:...127

To Mike, Nathan, Charles, Madilyn and Mei.
You are my why. I love you.

Opening Words

OUR LIFE EXPERIENCES SHAPE us. Our opinions, core values, and belief systems all come from the life we have lived and people we have interacted with. No individual can truly understand another because they haven't lived life through their eyes and perspective. This book is not any different. Our parenting story comes from our life experiences and choices we've made for our family.

On June 10, 1995, Mike and I joined hands for life. We brought to the table two different life experiences, and we had to meld our worlds into one. From that moment on, we started to create our own path together. There were certain life choices we decided to make in our marriage that would shape our family. For example, before we even had children we decided that we would do whatever it took for me to stay home with them while Mike was the sole income for us. Our parenting experiences cover the gamut of four children, homeschool, adoption, trauma, and sensory issues and we understand that not everyone will have the perspective we do. My vantage point of being a stay-at-home mom is not one that everyone will understand. If your family has never experienced a traumatic event, then you may not be able to identify with us in that area either.

Although we may not share the same experiences as the reader, I feel that our story carries some universal truths. God is good, kind, and gentle and he created us for choice and freedom. His desire is to draw us into relationship with him. Any parent in any stage of life should be able to connect with us on these truths as you read. No matter if you are a one- or two-income family or if you homeschool, have your children in public school, or are married or single, these truths should transfer to any family situation.

Our desire is that all will get to the end of this book and feel that you are not alone in the struggle that comes along with parenting. Our heart is that no parent feels condemned but will take a pause and think about how you are parenting and why. Finally, our hope is that you come away with a new-found resolution to model the heart of our heavenly Father to your children with gentleness and kindness.

• INTRODUCTION •

The Story Behind the Title

Sundays were crazy, busy days for us here at the Talley house. Mike and I both were on the leadership team at church, and we had to have the kids up and out of the door by 8:15 a.m. Most Sundays were easy, but not all. After years of this routine, our kids just thought it a part of life, but there were some Sundays that were more difficult than others.

One particular Sunday, our six-year-old had not slept well the night before and she was overtired and cranky. She was starting to dig in a little from the fact that she simply did not want to get dressed and go to church at 8:15 in the morning. I mean, I barely wanted to go myself seeing as I had been up with her most of the night. She couldn't find the outfit she wanted to wear, and frustration was setting in.

After going round and round with her with no budge in the right direction, I found myself sitting on her bed when I heard the Holy Spirit say, "She needs a choice." I sat there a moment and then asked her if she'd like a hug, to which she responded with a resounding, "Yes!" As she sat in my lap, her head on my chest, an idea for a choice dropped in my spirit. "Would you like to get dressed or wear pajamas to church?" I asked. She looked at me with those gorgeous almond eyes and said, "I can do that?" "Absolutely! Would you like to get dressed or wear pajamas to church?" I responded. Mei sat and thought for a minute, her head back on my chest. Her head popped up and then she exclaimed, "I choose pajamas!" I asked her if she wanted to wear the ones she had on or choose new ones. She chose the ones she had on. I asked her if she wanted to wear her tennis shoes or flip-flops. She chose tennis shoes. I asked her if she wanted cereal for breakfast or eggs. She chose cereal. She then hopped down and put her tennis shoes on, ate her cereal and proudly wore her pajamas to church that Sunday morning.

This is how we rolled at the Talley house when they were little. Even now with teens and adult kids, choices are the base of our parenting. All Mei needed in that moment was to take back a little bit of the control she felt she had lost. We shared it. She felt powerful in her decision. She felt heard when I gave her a choice. I knew she was exhausted. I knew she was struggling to manage her emotions and I simply gave her options, so she didn't feel so pinned in. By presenting her with one simple choice, I was able to affirm her tiredness and make her feel powerful so she could choose to shift her attitude.

Choices are incredibly powerful. We were created as free beings from the very beginning when God breathed life into Adam. He could have created us as automaton robots that had to obey his every command, but that's not what he wanted. He wanted us to have the ability to choose him. Such a risky move on God's part. There is something in each and every one of us that craves to operate in the gift that God gave us. We are wired for choice.

This book is about how Mike and I created a culture of freedom in our house. Freedom is a big gift to manage and allowing our children to make mistakes and learn to manage their freedom when they were younger has helped them to be able to think through the more costly decisions as they have gotten older. It's about learning as a parent that I cannot control my kids. Period. I can manipulate them into obedience or scare them into submission, but that's not the Father's heart at all. The heart of this book is about using the power of choice to share control. It's about doing away with cookie cutter parenting and learning to parent the individual child based on their needs in the moment. Finally, and most importantly, this book is about representing our heavenly Father to our children so they can ultimately keep their hearts connected to Him.

Parenting has been the most fun, aggravating, terrifying, and satisfying season of our lives. The responsibility is overwhelming sometimes, yet the joy of it all brings us to tears. This is our journey of learning to love our children the way God loves us and doing our best to lead them with gentleness and kindness.

I wrote the following in 2017 when the kids were seventeen, fifteen, thirteen, and ten. It pretty much sums up the roller coaster that is parenting in our house. I wouldn't trade these years for anything.

Sometimes we have grace.
Sometimes we have to say sorry.
Sometimes we have it all together.
Sometimes life hits us sideways.
Sometimes we experience loss.
Sometimes trauma affects the whole family.
Sometimes we laugh until we're in tears.
Sometimes we can't catch our breath.
Sometimes love wins.
Sometimes we give crazy choices.
Sometimes dreams come true.
Sometimes we miss them being little.
Sometimes the devil gets the best of us.
Sometimes we love them being big.
Sometimes we cheer them on.
Sometimes we pray them through.
Sometimes we have the answers.
Sometimes we don't sleep.
Sometimes we hold them.
Sometimes we let them.
Sometimes we share.
Sometimes we don't have the words.
Sometimes hearts get broken.
Sometimes we choose family over responsibilities.
Sometimes we embarrass them.
Sometimes we yell.
Sometimes tears are all we have to give.
Sometimes we dance wildly.

Sometimes we sing loudly.
Sometimes we cry over spilled milk.
Sometimes we can't find our clothes.
. . . . Sometimes we wear pajamas to church.

• CHAPTER 1 •

Sometimes It Comes Down to Relationship

"Kindness costs us nothing."
—Mike Talley

Parenting is hard. The End.

We had no idea when we decided to add children to our mix. We had zero clue that parenting could stretch us to our end. We never gave it a thought that this sweet, cuddly, little baby we brought home from the hospital would grow up and have their own opinions or that we would feel the weight of the responsibility that guiding an infant to adulthood would carry. We hadn't given any thought to how we would parent. We did not sit down and have a serious conversation about parenting styles. The only conversation we had was, "Do you want to have kids one day?" and when one day came, we started making babies. Not sure if it was naïve or brilliant that we didn't give much thought to any of it. Sometimes I think there is too much overthinking and way less closing your eyes, holding hands, and just taking the leap.

Our leap into parenthood started in 1999 with the devastating loss of our first baby. The excitement of our first pregnancy was met with so much heartache and grief. We were hit sideways with our first experience together with such great loss. To this day we still feel the sting of never getting to meet her. Clinging to each other and to the Lord, we kept moving forward and, before we knew it, we were pregnant again with our Nathan. Between 2000 and 2004, we had our first three children, Nathan, Charles, and Madilyn. By late 2004, we were talking about adding to our family in a different way and decided to adopt from China. We flew all the way across the world to get our fourth and final child, Mei, in January 2008.

Although we hadn't given much thought to parenting before we started having children, once they started coming along, we quickly learned that we did have some opinion how we wanted to parent moving forward. We were on the same page for the most part. We both valued authority, respectfulness, and obedience and worked to require these things from our children. I would say the only difference for me was that a peaceful home was high on my list of values, whereas, for Mike, it was not. We started to see stark differences in how we wanted to go about gaining this obedience and respect from our children.

My approach was one of softness and patience. I tried to approach them with kindness and gentleness. I wasn't always successful, but it felt more natural for me to keep a calm and peaceful demeanor. I had a more laid-back approach to parenting. A house of peace was top priority and so that's the atmosphere I tried to create for them. The only time I felt the need to exert my authority was in public places. Mike and I both felt the pressure to make sure our children were towing the line, especially in public. Making sure our children were perfect little angels in front of others was top priority. I personally put myself and my children under so much stress in these times and my peace would fly out the window. Appearances were everything. Other opinions started to guide my parenting style and I increasingly found myself operating from a place of fear.

It was around this time that I started asking internal questions about the whys behind my actions. Why do we make kids do things that most adults don't do? Why do we make our kids eat things they don't like? Why do we require impossible standards? Why can't children have a bad moment or day without punishment? Adults have bad attitudes all the time and we say they are just having a bad day. As I asked these questions, I started to see the double standard of how we treat children versus how we treat adults. It was the beginning of a big revelation for me and my approach to my children. I didn't want my kids to grow up in an environment where they were seen and not heard. I didn't want my fear of what others thought to guide my parenting choices.

Mike's approach to parenting was the polar opposite of mine. Mike describes his parenting approach as having a Dad voice, getting scary and yelling to gain the obedience and respect he was looking for. He had a "my way or the highway" approach to parenting when the kids weren't listening very well. He wanted unquestioning obedience for no other reason than "because I said so." Being in control was top priority for him because that feeling of being out of control was terrifying. With two different parenting styles going on, we weren't always on the same page. We both had the same values, but completely different approaches to getting there. Because we had such different approaches, it started to create a tension between us at times. I would think he was being too harsh and he would think I was being too easygoing. We struggled to find a compromise to be on the same page as far as setting the parenting tone in the house.

In January 2006, we, along with two other friend couples, went to a relationship conference in Brunswick, Georgia. We had never heard of the speakers before, but they came highly recommended to us. We were always on board with how we could improve our marriage. We had no idea that this one conference would turn our parenting world upside down. Danny Silk, author of *Loving Our Kids on Purpose*, along with his wife, Sheri, shared with us a new way of looking at parent–child relationships. Danny and Sheri were just starting out with their relationship ministry at the time. Danny came from a background of social work, counseling, and pastoring. He and Sheri shared testimony of how they struggled for years in their marriage until they gained the tools to communicate and the skills to build connection.

The Silks presented a view of relationships that we had

never given thought to. With 1 Corinthians 13:1–3 as their biblical basis, they explained how we are absolutely nothing without love.

> If I could speak all the languages of the earth and of angels, but didn't love others, I would only be a noisy gong or a clanging cymbal. If I had the gift of prophecy, and if I understood all of God's Secret plans and possessed all knowledge, and if I had such faith that I could move mountains, but didn't love others, I would have nothing. If I gave everything to the poor and even sacrificed my body, I could boast about it; but if I didn't Love others, I would have gained nothing. (NLT)

We learned that every interaction we have in our relationships must have love at the core. They wove this thought into 1 John 4:18.

> Such love has no fear, because perfect love expels all fear. If we are afraid, it is for fear of punishment, and this shows that we have not fully experienced his perfect love. (NLT)

Love and fear cannot coexist. Light bulbs started to go off for Mike and his parenting style as he read this scripture verse in a new light. He realized that he had been parenting from a place of fear, not love.

The number one revelation that we both got from the

Silks was that we cannot control anyone. Not even our kids. I remember one pivotal moment for me was when Danny Silk said, "On a good day I can tell myself what to do and actually do it." If we can't control ourselves on a consistent daily basis, why would we expect it of others? Why would we expect that of our children who are not developmentally mature? "Put a gun to my head and tell me to deny Christ, I still have a choice." They tied up the end of the conference in a nice little bow stringing all the scriptures and thoughts together. If control equals fear, then freedom equals love. Control is the outward expression of fear. That means the other side of that coin is also true; freedom is the outward expression of love. The opposite of control is freedom, and the opposite of fear is love.

This right here is where we both, in one moment, looked at each other and said we've got to do this differently. We can't go home now and do life as usual. When they started to talk about parent–child relationship, something that can only be described as a Holy Spirit encounter happened to both of us. It was the single most mind-transforming encounter either of us had ever experienced. The Silks talked about how they parented their children by giving them choices and teaching them to think. It had never occurred to us that in order not to be controlling of our children, we needed to give them choices. We went in one way and came out completely convicted with a new revelation on how to do life with our kids. Most importantly, the Lord started to reveal himself to us in a new way.

Danny and Sheri presented a new way for us to view our

heavenly Father. The verse "Train up a child in the way he should go . . ." took on a whole new meaning as we applied it to how God views and guides us. This verse does not say to train up a child in the way *I think* they should go. It says to train up a child in the way HE should go. I may have my view of how I think they should go, but what does God say about them? What is God's plan for them? How does God love them? God loves us all as individuals. He made us with our own personalities, needs, and wants. He guides us with these things in mind. He doesn't control or demand anything. He wants a relationship and out of that flows obedience and respect. Our minds were blown. God doesn't control, he guides us from a place of relationship and connection. Before we left, we asked Danny and Sheri to pray for us. We were headed home to our three children (at the time) with this brand-new way of doing things. We also were headed back to a church and friend culture where we would be alone in this way of parenting. They covered us in prayer, laying hands on us, asking the Lord to forever seal in us what we had learned that weekend.

We went home convinced that there was a more excellent way to show love to our children. We bought the Silks' DVD series called *Directing Vision Daily* and probably watched it fifteen times. At the end of the series, they flashed Danny Silk's email address to which we used often to ask questions about how to do this new way of parenting. One particular incident, our two-year-old, Madilyn, had been caught pinning her older brothers and their two friends against the wall in their room as she chunked toys at them. And I might add she was laughing hysterically. Mike emailed Danny asking for help for some advice on how to guide our two-year-old. I will never forget the first line of his response, "Wow! Sounds like she is going to be a world changer!" He proceeded to give us some ways we could parent her with choices. With the help of Danny from time to time we started to structure our house around relationship, honor, kindness, and love. We tried to put choice, not control, as the center of our parenting moving forward.

So, how did we take this revelation and apply it in our home? Well, for one, we had to make a choice to view God differently. We started to realize that he is not some big guy in the sky waiting to whack us every time we make a wrong choice. He is a kind, gentle God constantly guiding our hearts from a place of relationship. Next, we had to start mirroring our new view of God to our children. Practically speaking, that looked like kindness and grace extended as well as introducing choices as a way of parenting. And, finally, it looked like letting go of external motivation to steer our children and working on heart connection through relationship to help guide them.

Relationship

God doesn't want robots. He wants a relationship. Adam and Eve walked in the garden with Him in the cool of the day. Abraham is called a friend of God. David is called a man after God's heart. Jesus modeled relationship with his disciples and with the Father. The Bible constantly points to the importance of relationship. Relationship with others and relationship with God are woven into the story of redemption.

We were created to be free beings. Let's start there. God wove it into the beginning of our story as he created us. After God created Adam he told him to name the animals. He didn't tell him what to name the animals. He gave Adam that choice. Adam and Eve had the choice to eat or not eat of the forbidden fruit. Cain chose to offer a subpar offering to God, thus, leading him down a road where he chose to murder his brother. God knew that free will could lead to us choosing poorly, but in his goodness and wisdom he decided he'd rather have his most beautiful creation choose to love him than require it by force. Over and over again, he proves to us that he is not afraid of our choices. He mourns with us when we choose poorly. He allows the natural consequences of our choices to play out. He walks beside us, always, and points us in the right direction, but it's our choice to take the right path or not. God is more concerned about what is going on in our hearts. He desires a true relationship with us.

He cultivated this idea of relationship with us starting in the Garden of Eden. In the garden, after Adam and Eve had sinned, God comes looking for them.

> Then the man and his wife heard the sound of the Lord God as he was walking in the garden in the cool of the day, and they hid from the Lord God among the tress of the garden. But the Lord

> God called to the man, "Where are you?" (Genesis 3:8–9, NIV)

The creator of the universe came and walked in the garden with them in the cool of the day desiring to be among his creation. He knew they were hiding, but he also knew where they were. He even knew what they did. He didn't have to ask, "Where are you?", but he did out of relationship with them. He desired to hear what they had to say.

It reminds me of when I used to play hide and seek with my kids. I knew they are hiding, and I knew exactly where they were, yet I interacted with them and yelled through the house, "Where is Mei! Has anyone seen Mei? I can't find her! Oh, there you are!" I would go through these motions because I love my daughter and wanted to draw her closer in a relationship with me. I got on her level. I feel that in that moment, when God saw that they had sinned and went to walk in the garden, he was getting on their level. He talked and listened to them when he really did not have to. He could have just banished them with no explanation. After they confessed their sin, he loved and cared for them enough to make them clothes before he sent them on their way. Relationship has always been the goal.

Abraham is known as a friend of God. My favorite verse about Abraham is in Genesis 18:20–32, when he has this whole interaction with God and ends up "changing God's mind."

> **20** Then the Lord said, "The outcry against Sodom and Gomorrah is so great and their sin so

grievous **21** that I will go down and see if what they have done is as bad as the outcry that has reached me. If not, I will know."

22 The men turned away and went toward Sodom, but Abraham remained standing before the Lord. **23** Then Abraham approached him and said: "Will you sweep away the righteous with the wicked? **24** What if there are fifty righteous people in the city? Will you really sweep it away and not spare the place for the sake of the fifty righteous people in it? **25** Far be it from you to do such a thing—to kill the righteous with the wicked, treating the righteous and the wicked alike. Far be it from you! Will not the Judge of all the earth do right?"

26 The Lord said, "If I find fifty righteous people in the city of Sodom, I will spare the whole place for their sake." (NIV)

Abraham and God gave this whole back and forth and each time Abraham is asking for the Lord to spare the city for the sake of less and less righteous people. Eventually, Abraham is down to just ten righteous people.

32 Then he said, "May the Lord not be angry, but let me speak just once more. What if only ten can be found there?"

He answered, "For the sake of ten, I will not destroy it."

33 When the Lord had finished speaking with Abraham, he left, and Abraham returned home. (NIV)

Why did God feel the need to share anything with Abraham at all? Why did the Lord let Abraham question him? Why did God seemingly change his mind and spare Lot and his family? Genesis 19:29 says because "God remembered Abraham." Once again, the God of the universe demonstrates his desire for us to commune and interact with him. He cares about our thoughts and desires and, yes, he knows the outcome of every choice we could possibly make, but that doesn't matter to him. He finds joy in the interaction regardless.

Heart connection and relationship are 100% vital to the way we do life with our children. If my heart is healthily connected to my child, then that relationship is as such that we don't want to hurt the other with our actions or behavior. I've been there when I've let my emotions take over and I go into behavior management mode, but I promise the most meaningful heart changes have happened when I take a minute to connect to my child's heart before we address behavior. That may look like acknowledging the obvious. "You seem so angry." "I'm so sorry you are frustrated." "Do you need a hug?"

When emotions are high, nobody is listening or receiving information. Sometimes taking a second to address and affirm the emotion first will bring a calming to the situation.

Connecting with your child's heart sends them the message that they are loved and seen first and foremost. Out of relationship with my child, I will always desire to be kind, honoring, and loving to them above all else and vice versa. Just as our relationship with our heavenly Father should be. I honor and obey the Lord because I value the relationship we have, and I don't want to grieve his heart. He is loving, gentle, and kind to me because he values and loves me unconditionally.

Honor
One of the major goals Mike and I have made as parents is to always remember that our relationship with our children is built on love and honor. Honor needs to be the foundation of any relationship, but to pull that concept into our parenting was a big shift for us. Some people may think of honor as something that is always shown to those in authority over us. For example, a child honoring their parents. But what if honor is supposed to first be modeled? What does it look like to honor your children before tackling it that other way around? Our plumb line is our heavenly Father. How does he love us? How does he treat us? Is he harsh? Is he punishing?

He is a good and loving God who will never give us a stone if we ask for bread. He will wait on the porch and watch the horizon. He is slow to anger. He loves extravagantly. These are the attributes we get to show our children. We get to be an extension of the Father to them so that, ultimately, they will want to cultivate a relationship with him.

Children learn by watching. They learn by mimicking the

world around them. If you are modeling honor in your home, children will follow your lead. So, what does that look like for us? It looks like kindness with our words and tone. It looks like letting our children have a voice. It looks like extending grace and understanding. It looks like correcting gently and managing ourselves even when the kids aren't doing the same. If I want to require honor in my home, I first must get that down myself. I can't expect something from my children that I'm not able to model for them. Jesus took time to model honor for us when he washed the disciples' feet. He had formed such a close relationship with each and every one of them. They had been through a whirlwind three years of ministry together and with deep conversations and crazy signs and wonders. He had created a bond like no other with them. In this humbling, sweet moment the King of kings forever sealed in our hearts what it looks like when honor flows from the top down.

When our children were young, Mike and I went through a one-year school of ministry at our church. For nine months, we spent every Monday and Tuesday evening from 6 p.m. to 9 p.m. up at the church. Three of the kids were in school at the time so we would bring air mattresses for them to sleep on so they could keep somewhat of a schedule. Nine months and they never once complained. At the end of the year, on ministry school graduation night, we decided to honor our children for their sacrifice. We brought them up to the front and gushed about how amazing they were to have given their Monday and Tuesday nights up for Mom and Dad. We told them we wanted to honor them and presented them with the gift of a brand-new Wii in front of all the others in attendance.

It was a purposeful, teachable moment for our children. Showing honor to our children sent the message to them that their selfless sacrifice was seen. They weren't expecting it. The thought of a reward had never crossed their minds. They were perfectly content with us verbally telling them how proud we were of them, which we had done often that whole year; but, when we physically showed them honor, it blessed them on a different level. Mom and Dad, their authority, took time to make sure they were seen.

Kindness

Kindness costs us nothing. It's free. It can go a long way to ensuring connection with my child. Yes, even in frustrating times. Especially when they are being unkind to us. Is it hard? Oh, my goodness, yes! When I have a disrespectful child in front of me, the very last thing I am thinking about is being kind a lot of the time. I have to remind myself who I am representing to them. In that moment, who do I want them to see? An irate mom who has lost her ever-loving mind because she is over the back talk? Or a mom who can manage her emotions well and still show the heart of the Father in the midst of her child's "unloveliness"? I try to remind myself that they are kids and I'm the adult. I have had way more practice at managing my emotions and learning how to communicate my needs and wants. I don't want to create a disconnect with my tone or words. That won't lead to anywhere good.

A prime example is my response to Mei in the "Sometimes

We Wear Pajamas to Church" story. She was being less than cooperative, and I could have matched her frustration at that moment (as I had in past moments of frustration), but I chose to look at her with compassion and respond with kindness. It changed everything.

Choose kindness. It can dismantle a disrespectful situation swiftly and leave everyone intact. I love what Romans 2:4 says about God and what his kindness does for us, "Don't you see how wonderfully kind, tolerant, and patient God is with you? Does this mean nothing to you? Can't you see that his kindness is intended to turn you from your sin?"

If his kindness towards us can lead me toward repentance, then my kindness to my children should do the same.

Love

It may seem sort of obvious to say that love is also a key to staying connected to your child. It's like, "Duh, of course, I have to love my kid," but what if it's so much more than just something we say. What if it's a way of life? What if love really is the number one way to keep that connection we have with our child? Love requires an action. It requires a laying down of myself or a dying to myself for these humans that are in my care. It means I manage myself when they are out of control. It means I show them how to own mistakes by saying I'm sorry when I've hurt them. It means I listen when they speak even if it's not delivered perfectly. It means I correct them with a kind and gentle tone. It means I lead them by their hand sometimes, but by their heart always. Love shines a light on the things they need to work on. It shows understanding and grace in the moment they are in, yet says, "I want to see you grow into all you are meant to be, will you let me help you?" Love doesn't force its way in. Love is safety they can feel. Love is creating a space for them to fail. Love is getting sad with them when they do. I could go on and on. It all comes down to love. Unconditionally showing them the Father's heart over and over again.

Gah, I'm weeping as I write this part because if my kids come out as adults knowing even a fraction of how much the Father loves them, I will feel that I've succeeded. With all my failures, and there have been many, I simply want them to know how much love he has for them. That he's there for them and never leaves them. He is their safe place. He cheers with them and weeps with them. He is after their heart above all else and he is good Father.

As parents, it is our responsibility to set the tone of our household. Do we want to create an atmosphere of love, kindness, and gentleness where choice and relationship are valued? Or, do we want to create an atmosphere of fear and control where we use external motivation just to get our kids to comply? I've parented both ways and both will get the job done as far as parenting goes, but one points to relationship as key and the other points to control as key. Our heavenly Father loves us. Control has never been in his nature. Love and control cannot remotely coexist. If I'm going to model how God does relationship with us then I have to throw control out the window and choose love and relationship as my parenting guide.

• CHAPTER 2 •

Sometimes We Parent from Our Pain—Mike Talley

"Parenthood? What neighborhood is that?"
—Charles (age 10)

FROM THE MOMENT WE are born and begin experiencing the world, our body, mind, and soul begin to take notes. We begin to associate our daily encounters with emotions: joy, fear, worry, laughter, love, safety, etc. Both good and bad experiences are given a memory and an emotion and filed away, deep into our very being. When we encounter our friendly grandmother, our brain looks for the emotion that it coded for this encounter and returns *smiles, excitement,* and *love.* When we encounter an angry dog that looks like the dog that bit us years ago, our brain finds the coded emotion and returns *fear, run away,* and *panic.* When we encounter a stressful situation that reminds us of that time when Dad was super angry and scary, our brain finds the coded emotion and returns *fear, insecurity, low self-worth,* and *control*. This is because every interaction we have with our world from the moment we are born until the moment we die is written in our codebook.

Close to ten years ago, one of my pastors recommended that I watch a teaching on communication. The teaching was by Dann Farrelly, a pastor at Bethel Church Redding in California, called *Brave Communication*. I watched the teaching over and over again because I have always struggled to effectively communicate. Oh, I could communicate, but it was rarely effective and usually produced less than happy results. I personally recommend you this teaching, that you purchase it and watch it over and over again. It has been life-changing for me, even though I am still very much a work in progress. Dann began the discussion on communication by describing something he calls the "Codebook." The reason he started with this topic is because how we process our surroundings is largely dictated by what is written in our codebook. If you are to become better at communicating, you have to know what is in your codebook. Once you know and understand this, you can then begin to rewrite your book.

Your codebook defines you. It takes every interaction and assigns emotions and memories. Your brain will access these emotions and memories when you encounter situations that are similar to past experiences. If it is a new experience, your brain will file away a new emotion and memory for retrieval later.

This is all great for communication, but why is it in this book and why is it in this chapter? The reason is because you

WILL parent from your codebook. In some cases, this isn't necessarily a bad thing. Good memories and emotions are very helpful as a parent. Encountering situations with your children that bring up the happy/healthy memories means that you will most likely respond in positive, constructive ways. However, encountering situations with your children that bring up past pain/trauma/unhealthy memory means that you will most likely respond in negative, destructive ways.

We all have levels of trauma in our life. What Jen and I have noticed is that when a traumatic event happens in a family, every sibling and parent will view and process that trauma differently. For some, it becomes a life-defining moment that they struggle to move past the rest of their lives. For others, it may have been a dark moment in their life, but they have not let the trauma impact their life. Then the rest of us are somewhere in between.

The current popular word for this is *triggering*. But why do we trigger? It all goes back to your codebook. *Triggering* is simply your brain/body trying to figure out how to respond when presented with a situation like other unpleasant or traumatic experiences in our life. We all act like we don't have a codebook, but we all do, and each book is vastly different from everyone else's book. It is important to learn about your codebook because you will bring your book with you into marriage and into parenting.

When you get married, you bring your codebook and your spouse brings theirs. The problem is we both believe that we have the same book. This is why you will say and hear the statement, "Everyone knows that!" Yeah, no; actually, everyone doesn't know that. YOU know that because you experienced something that your brain assigned an emotion and a memory to. Your spouse may have experienced a similar thing in their life, yet their brain assigned a totally different emotion and memory. This conflict between codebooks is a cause of many marital issues. The codebook conflict impacts mundane, seemingly insignificant issues: what does a clean house look like, when is the trash full (Dann Farrelly has a funny story on this), how to wash clothes, how to make a certain food dish, how to dress, how to host social events. The conflict also impacts very important issues: how to handle money, how to do conflict resolution, and how to parent.

Way back in 1995, when Jen and I got married, she would talk to me about combining our normals. We both came to our marriage with what we considered normal. This normal was based on our individual codebooks, which we have discussed are not the same. We had to combine our normals into one, new Talley family normal. As with most marriages, this was not always easy and was the subject of many disagreements and fights. After all, I came from a very quiet, reserved family with only two siblings and a divorced mom and dad. She came from a loud, energetic family with both parents and three very different siblings. Thankfully, we found lots of common ground and began to lay the groundwork for what we wanted our family's normal to look like.

Jen and I have largely been on the same page when it comes to parenting. We both were impacted by the relationship conference she spoke of in chapter 1 and came home and decided to change how we were parenting. The only problem was that neither of us had dealt very much with our codebooks. As a result, often our parenting was colored by negative entries in our books. This caused us to react in ways that caused negative entries into our kids' codebooks.

I believe there are only two base emotions: love and fear. I am not a psychologist, so it's possible I am wrong, but it seems that all other emotions flow from these two. Anger and control are just fear verbalized or acted out. Peace and contentment flow from a position of love. In parenting, when we encounter situations that bring us fear, then most likely our codebook is going to spit out anger and control. Similarly, when we encounter positive parenting experiences, then most likely our codebook is going to spit out affirming, loving emotions. Parenting from the good aspects of our codebook is the best way and, if we all did that, then this chapter would not be necessary. Unfortunately, we all have a natural inclination to parent from our pain when faced with circumstances that trigger our pain.

Growing up, I was a very fearful kid who worried about everything. My brain learned how to deal with fear and worry by developing coping mechanisms. Most of the time these were not the most constructive mechanisms. Out of my fear, I desired to control my surroundings. After all, if I could control my surroundings, then I could prevent people and circumstances from hurting me. When I felt out of control I would eat, listen to dark music, retreat into myself, and engaged in a myriad of other self-destructive behaviors. Unfortunately, all of this did not magically disappear when I became a parent. Now, I was faced with four little kids who could get sick, make bad choices, be hurtful, or be unpredictable. All those things brought me anxiety and fear. After the relationship conference, I finally understood that I could not control a single one of those possibilities, and that scared me to death. The last sixteen or so years have been a journey to deal with my underlying fear and control issues. It has not been easy and there have been many hurt hearts along the way, but I keep working on cleaning up my codebook. As Dann Farrelly says in *Brave Communication*, I need to learn how to properly respond when I hear or have a strong emotion. If you are a parent, hearing and having strong emotions is a daily occurrence.

Instead of just talking about this concept, I wanted to provide some examples of when I parented out of my pain. You may be thinking, nah, this isn't an issue for me. I hope that is the case, but most of us struggle with this issue. I hope maybe some of these examples will help you see or remember instances when you, too, parented from your pain. We like to say that children know how to push our buttons. All that means is that kids, knowingly or unknowingly, hit our undealt with trigger points and we react.

My wife and kids call me Mr. Safety. Especially when the kids were young, I was constantly on the lookout for potential dangers that could impact my children. This isn't necessarily a bad thing, and some would say it's just part of parenting. I would agree with that statement, but mine was driven by fear.

Out of my fear, I sought to control the kid's environment. It got so bad that I would do the same for other people's kids. Sometimes it was my nieces and nephews, but I would even do this to complete stranger's kids. Everything that COULD be a potential danger made me nervous and anxious. The result was that I would bark orders and issue warnings to everyone: "Hey, watch that over there; be careful with that; that looks dangerous; hey, Jen, should they be there; oh no, someone might get hurt." Instead of parenting by coming alongside my kids and gently teaching them to pay attention to certain things, I was a nervous Nellie, issuing orders and being anxious all the time. I have learned that when I am anxious, my kids pick up on it and it makes them anxious as well.

Many years ago, Jen pointed out that I physically responded to frustration and worry in ways that were visible to everyone. I had no idea, but apparently, I give off three different visual clues that I am frustrated or worried: the long blink, the sigh, and the smirk. Usually, two are bundled together; and, if I am very frustrated, you are likely to get all three at once. My kids have written these three visual cues into their codebooks. It is likely that if they encounter a situation where someone they love does one of those three things, they will think the person is frustrated with them. It is possible that the person is frustrated, but it's also just as likely that they are not frustrated. Maybe that is how they think through a problem or the face they make when they are tired. But my kids have learned that when someone long blinks, sighs, or smirks, then that person is frustrated with them. Now that I know I am doing this, I am working on not wearing my emotions on my face. It has actually become a joke in our house when I do it. Especially when I do it to Jen. She will say, "Don't you long blink me!"

When my kids behave in a way or make choices that cause me fear, my go-to emotion has been anger. This is usually exhibited by a combination of raising my voice, outright yelling, and lecturing. When the boys were around twelve and fourteen years old, they were wrestling. Nate picked up Charles and "Superman-ed" him into the kitchen table. The impact broke one of Charles' teeth. It was a jagged break that definitely needed dental work. I allowed fear to immediately take over me. All I could think about was the cost of root canals, crowns, and implants. To be honest, I was in a full-on panic. My mind raced through all the possibilities. It was a weekend and we couldn't get to the dentist for over a day. What if he stated having severe pain? I remembered when Jen had suffered terribly from a weekend toothache. What if he needed major dental work? I didn't have dental insurance. I didn't have any savings.

In my fear, I reacted very negatively. I took a simple accident, one where the boys were just playing, and I turned it into a major codebook entry for Nate. I took him outside and told him how irresponsible he had been, that this was going to cost thousands of dollars, and that he needed to be more responsible. I remember I was shaking all over as I said those words. But the words were said and the damage was done. I noticed a change in Nate after that. He did become more responsible after that, but not in a good way. He started to become Mr. Safety himself. He had a new entry in his codebook.

Roughhousing was irresponsible. Someone could get hurt and cost lots of money. Big parent fail and a prime example of parenting from your pain. I was scared because we grew up in a family where money was tight. I was acutely aware that when I was irresponsible, I could cost us money. I don't remember a specific event that made me fear costing my family money, but it got into my book. If I could do that night over, I would pull Nate aside, put my arms around him, and tell him, "Man, I know that was scary, but Charlie is going to be OK. You did nothing wrong. You were just playing with your brother. I am sorry he got hurt and I am sorry if it scared you, but don't worry, it's all OK." Just think of the positive codebook entry that would have been . . . sadly it wasn't what happened.

There were countless examples of me losing my cool due to hearing disrespect from my children. Should disrespect be addressed? Absolutely! But it needs to be in a way that strengthen and helps my connection with the kid who is being disrespectful. Oddly enough, yelling and lecturing do not seem to have a very positive outcome. Yet, when I hear disrespect, I want to react out of my fear. Again, I am not sure when that particular entry entered my book, but it's a struggle at times.

Another time, Charles had done something that ultimately made me worry. It was either his behavior or the words that he said, but I got anxious and decided to lecture him. The lecture was bad enough, but it got louder and louder. Finally, Charles looked at me and said, "You don't have to be so harsh, Dad." It broke me. He was right. I could share my worry about his behavior and words in a much more constructive way.

If like us, you have struggled with parenting out of your pain, what should you do? The best advice I can give anyone, parent or not, is to work on yourself. Get help! See a therapist. Talk to your pastor. Talk to someone you trust. The important point is to talk about it. Find out what triggers your fear and work on constructive ways to rewrite that section of your codebook. You will never undo a lifetime of learned experiences, but you can choose to do things differently. Will you mess up? Yep! But you keep working, keep trying to heal. Our kids deserve a healthy mom and dad. But this also doesn't mean that you need to have all your crap together before becoming a parent. You will never get there. It is most important to understand you have issues from your past and that those issues can impact your parenting. Once you understand this, you can get help from books, a therapist, or friends. The goal isn't perfection, it is being healthier today than yesterday.

It is also very important to clean up past messes with your kids. Looking back, Jen and I can point to different instances where we blew it. We will say, "Yeah, that one will come up in therapy one day." It is not to belittle or make light of the mother/father wound we gave our child, but it is the recognition that we blew it. We have found that a wonderful way to honor our children is to admit when we mess up and to seek their forgiveness. At the end of the day, I don't want my kids to idolize me. I want them to know that their dad was human and made lots of mistakes but that he loved me enough and was humble enough to own up to those mistakes. It may have been years ago that you parented out of your pain or you may be reminded of a specific event. Go to your kids and admit you were wrong and ask for their forgiveness. This is such a healthy way to build connection with your kids. For the tooth story I mentioned above, it was years later that the Lord convicted me of how I handled that night. Nate and Ary were over one night for dinner. He and I were standing at the grill, and I finally got my nerve up to tell him I was so sorry for that night and I am sorry that I taught him a bad lesson. He looked at me and said, "Not to take anything away from what you said, but I have already dealt with all of that; of course, I forgive you." Just writing that makes me want to cry. My humility and honesty with my son, even years later helped build our connection. A few Father's Days ago, I had all the kids around the table and I asked for forgiveness for parenting from my pain. I had allowed the various traumas from my childhood to impact my parenting, which impacted them. It was a very special moment where I was able to share my heart of repentance to the kids and they were able to extend forgiveness to me.

We are all a work in progress. Have grace for yourself and understand you did not become who you are overnight, so it may take some time. But admit your issues and seek help. This book is not a self-help book or seminar, but there are many out there. A few I suggest are: *Brave Communication*—Dann Farrelly, *The Supernatural Power of Forgiveness*—Kris and Jason Vallotton, *Unpunishable: Ending Our Love Affair with Punishment*—Danny Silk, and *Victorious Emotions: Creating a Framework for a Happier You*—Wendy Backlund.

• CHAPTER 3 •

Sometimes We Correct

"Raising kids is like raising plants.
You are supposed to nurture them and help them grow."
—Mei (age 15)

DISCIPLINE IS PROBABLY ONE of the most controversial topics in the parenting world. There have been so many debates on the best way to correct children. It's a heavy topic that can leave parents feeling ashamed and confused. Most debates I've heard are always based on the best method of which we can control our children. The problem I have with these methods are that they are devoid of a path for connection and relationship. Correction should always lead to connection. One of the first things that Mike and I did when we got back from that conference was to change the way we discipline our children. With the goal of relationship in mind, we started to find ways to correct our children while still maintaining a heart connection with them. We wanted to guide them not yank them along through life. We wanted to find a way to correct our children that reflected the Father's heart and that would lead to connection not compliance.

We started to study Jesus and his interactions with those around him. We found that Jesus had an amazing ability to have compassion and mercy and still hold the standard. An example of this is in John 8:1–11, when he addresses the issue of the woman caught in adultery. By law she deserved to be stoned to death, but Jesus released mercy into the situation and then told her to "go and sin no more." Jesus led his disciples by example. He showed them how to treat children when he drew the children close to himself, held them, and blessed them in Mark 10:13–15. He showed them how to treat sinners and tax collectors then drew them into his world and ate with them in Luke 15:1–2. Jesus was not about condemnation or leading with an iron fist. He didn't expect his followers to do anything he hadn't already done. Jesus was the ultimate servant leader and he led by example.

Mike and I desired to lead our children the same way. We realized we wanted them to be kind to others, we needed to show them what kindness looks like in our everyday life. If we wanted them to be respectful, we needed that heart posture to them as well. If we want them to own their mistakes, we needed to not shy away from saying "I'm sorry" when we messed up. Good parent leadership meant we shifted to intentionally leading our children with gentleness and kindness.

Correction and discipline can take several paths in our house. It can look like redos, two-part conversations, or time in/outs. Always with the intent of a heart change in the end. All are intentional ways to correct behavior or heart issues. By intentional, I mean I am walking them through a process, not simply telling them to stop whatever behavior they are doing. These correction tools, so to speak, are the ones that have worked well with our family through the years, especially when they were young.

Redos

I had been reading books on childhood trauma and was looking for practical tips on how to parent such children when I ran across a book by Dr. Karen B. Purvis, Dr. David R. Cross, and Wendy Lyons Sunshine, *The Connected Child*. As I did more research on Purvis, I found that she also was responsible for developing Trust-Based Relational Intervention. Out of her research of adopted children, she and her colleague Dr. David Cross developed tools for connecting with children from hard places with behavior issues. All children, whether they are from a hard place or not, will struggle with self-regulating at one point or another. *Self-regulating* is defined as the ability to understand and manage your behavior and your reactions to feelings and the things that happen to you. This includes being able to manage emotions like frustration, anger, and excitement. It's the ability to control our words and bodies when we hear or feel strong emotions. Emotions can feel like giants that take over quickly and can come out ugly as a child or teen. It is my responsibility as a parent to guide them in this area and redos are a great tool.

One of the ways Purvis suggested to help curb behavior was through redoing behavior responses the correct way. For example, if my child hits another child because they are angry, I will first tell them we are kind with our hands and then walk them through redoing behavior by using their words not their hands. If my teen comes out of their room in the morning scratchy and ill at the world, I will tell them to try again. I have literally walked my child back their room and said, "Let's try again." This form of correction lets them know that their behavior wasn't acceptable, and it gives them a chance to do it correctly. I always say something like, "That's better!' or "Good job!" Then we move on. No lecturing, no yelling, no frustration.

Redos have been a game changer for us. There's something about relearning through positive connections that give our emotions and brains a chance to learn a better way of handling ourselves. Kids cannot self-regulate very well when they are young. Even some adults struggle with this as well. A child learning to self-regulate takes an enormous amount of practice on their part and so much patience on the parents' part.

Two-Part Conversations
Two-part conversations are a great tool for older children and teens. Sometimes the goal isn't just behavior-driven. Sometimes emotions are so high that two-part conversations are needed. The first part of the conversation is needed to help reconnect what's been disconnected, and the second part is to address behavior.

When my child is overcome with big feelings and they are struggling to regulate or manage themselves, sometimes disrespectful tone or words are spoken. Instead of addressing the disrespect right off the bat or getting myself on their emotional level (we call it *getting on their merry-go-round*), I take a minute to validate their feelings, offer a hug, or tell them I'm sorry they are sad, mad, disappointed, or whatever they are feeling in that moment. I will ask them if they can put words to their feelings, so I know how to help them navigate. We take deep breaths. We get that oxygen back up into their brain so they can think and reason. Offer a drink of water or a snack so they can start to shift to a less emotional state. So many behavior issues can be simply hunger or dehydration. I am reminded of the candy bar commercial with the raging football player who, when given a snack, turns into a sweet little old grandma. Hangry is a real thing and sometimes a snack is all it takes for self-regulation and clear thinking to kick in.

In these moments, I'm only thinking of reconnecting my heart to theirs. I am not addressing the behavior or disrespect. I'm not letting my emotions get tangled with theirs. I'm simply coming alongside them and sitting with them in the moment. Parents, this is probably one the most crucial parts of intentional parenting. If I want to see a true heart change in my kids, I first need to approach them with kindness and understanding. Yes, your toddler might be throwing a fit over not being able to have a toy. Yes, your second grader may be grumpy in the car after school. Yes, your middle schooler may be crying over a look you gave them. Yes, your teenager might slam their door when you asked them to clean their room. Your toddler may feel disappointed and can't get the words out to tell you. Your second grader may be exhausted, dehydrated, or simply hungry. Your middle schooler may be still hurting from a friend rejecting them earlier in the day. Your teen may have just told friends he was free to hang out and feels embarrassed he forgot to clean his room. There are always reasons behind behaviors. Connecting our hearts to theirs in these moments is the key to seeing them shift.

Once emotions are back in check, brains are thinking, and hearts are connected, then behavior can be addressed. Sometimes, that can look like tackling it right then, or it can look like waiting until the next day. For a toddler, behavior needs to be addressed immediately. Their brains aren't going to remember much past the moment and a redo can be done. For an elementary age child, a couple of hours may be needed to really make sure that they are in a place to receive and hear what you have to say. As far as teens go, it sometimes may have to be the next day and, just from my experience, my teens usually need some time to think and process. A lot of the times they will revisit the conversation themselves with us to either apologize or talk things out in a calmer manner and sometimes we, as parents, are the ones who have to initiate that second conversation. No one is in a place to listen when emotions are high, so take the time to be intentional with their heart first.

Time Ins/Outs

We generally used time ins and time outs when the kids were between the ages of eighteen months and six years old. We found them useful to help them pause to be able to think through and take ownership of the problem they were facing. Almost everyone has used or heard of *time out*. It's a method of letting your child have some time alone to calm down and think about the issue at hand. As with all children they all have different needs. My boys were able to handle time outs well. They had zero issue and it helped them tremendously to have some quiet alone time to think things over. My girls, on the other hand, became more stressed out and it had the opposite effect on them. Being left alone caused great anxiety and added to the issue. Self-regulation went out the window and it would have been beneficial if I had sat and held them while they processed and thought things over. One thing we learned is that if time outs add stress to the situation, then they are useless for any learning to happen. If our presence helped them to regain composure and remain calm, we would park ourselves right next to them or even hold them if they wanted. Both of these methods can start as early as eighteen months old. For children to be able to connect choice to consequence, they need the space to learn and to be given choices. We never set a time limit. We simply would ask if they were calm enough to manage themselves now or if they were ready to be fun. If "I'm sorry" or "I forgive you" needed to be said, then we would walk them through what that looked like and then move on with our day.

Intentional parenting with the goal of connection first

isn't the easiest path to take, but I promise if you put the work in with your child when they are young it will come to reap so much benefit when they are older. This heart connection that you are cultivating with them at a young age needs to be as strong as it possibly can be when they are teens and young adults. At some point, they will be making big kid choices that have big kid consequences and your relationship with them may be the thing that keeps them from making that choice that leads them down a hard road.

    Be kind. Be loving. Be honoring. Those three attributes will go a long way to staying connected to your child's heart for years to come.

• CHAPTER 4 •

Sometimes We Parent Differently

"Trauma doesn't happen in a vacuum. It impacts everyone within arm's length."
—Jen Talley

CHOICE-BASED PARENTING IS DEFINITELY our go-to parenting style for 90% of the time. It's effective in teaching children how to think and helps with teaching children to manage their emotions, but what if your child is in a state of mind where they can't think and they cannot manage their emotions? What if they are operating out of the survival part of their brain and it's all they can do to stay present? What if that part of the brain is in full-on protective mode and the only emotion that can be expressed is fear or, even worse, there is no room for emotion at all? This is where a parenting shift needs to happen.

The Talleys haven't been without trauma, unfortunately, and we soon realized that choices and consequences were not going to work on a child that's in a constant state of survival and always operating on a stress level of 15. It wasn't fair to them to treat them as they were completely fine and normal when the truth was they were not. Them living in a constant state of survival made it very difficult for them to connect to us on a parent–child level. When everything and everyone is perceived as threat, connection becomes almost impossible. Our decision to shift from choice-based to solely connection-based was a game changer for them and we've never regretted it. We started to see improvement and healing take place after about six months of this type of parenting. Healing started happening. Reasoning started to be restored. Emotions started to chill out and the ability to self-regulate started to return. It wasn't the easy route at all. It took a ton of patience and grace to walk through that season. It took me deep diving into childhood trauma and how it affects the brain and our emotions. A mountain of books read, trying new approaches, and lots of prayer, but we did it, and I'm here to tell you that it works.

Traumatic Events
One of the reasons a parent may need to parent differently is because of a traumatic event. It's so unfortunate and devastating when these happen. It can come in the form of bullying, medical emergencies, physical abuse, sexual abuse, emotional abuse, adoption, foster care, neglect, birthing trauma, and many others I haven't listed. When these events happen, our brains go into protective mode. The only part of the brain that is functioning is the amygdala, which is responsible for keeping us alive in times of danger. It's a primal place that our brain

goes to keep us alive. The only thing your brain is telling you to do is survive.

> "When a child experiences trauma, the child's ability to develop a sufficient regulatory system is severely compromised. In cases of severe trauma, the child's life is literally at risk. For these children, their internal survival mechanisms then become activated, dedicating all the body's resources to remain alert in 'survival mode.' These children perceive the world as threatening from a neurological, physical, emotional, cognitive, and social perspective. They operate from a paradigm of fear to ensure their safety and security." (Heather T. Forbes and B. Bryan Post, *Beyond Consequences, Logic, and Control*)

Neurotransmitters are the data messengers of our brain. The two main categories are the excitatory neurotransmitters (rev up our nervous system) and the inhibitory neurotransmitters (calm down our nervous system). These two are only helpful to us when they are in balance with one another. When there is an imbalance, we start to see things like mood swings and the inability to think clearly.

> "We've seen similarly distorted neurotransmitter profiles in children we work with for years after they have been adopted into secure homes. Even though they're living in a safe and

loving family environment, their neurochemistry can be wildly irregular. . . . The resulting neurotransmitter imbalances make it physically difficult for formerly harmed children to maintain a relaxed and happy mood and cause them to get easily excited and distressed." (*The Connected Child*)

This is where our fight-or-flight instincts take over. There are no number of choices and reasoning that will be able to take place when a person is in this state. A child who has been in a constant state of feeling unsafe can sometimes go years in this survival mode of living. We all see or even know these types of people. Their behaviors are irrational and sometimes dangerous. They cannot be reasoned with. Their decisions in life have been destructive or numbing in nature. They are living in a primal state of survival. When a child has suffered a trauma of any type, then we can start to understand why choice-based parenting will not work on a child in this state. There is no way a child can reason enough to make a choice if their brains are always in survival mode. The only function they have is to protect themselves. That can look like shutting down emotions or fighting for their life. My point is that parenting must look different for these kids until they are able to operate outside of survival mode.

"It was once said to me, 'Scary children do scary things.' The simple truth in this wise statement is that while we believe that children are perfectly capable of making clear and rational decisions, we also need to believe the opposite—that children are incapable of making clear and rational decisions." (*Beyond Consequences, Logic, and Control*) Sometimes, the weight of the world and the stress that trauma brings make it impossible for our children to behave rationally.

So, what does parenting look like for the traumatized child? It looks like making purposeful and positive connections. Heather T. Forbes says, "Parenting a child with traumatic history is about learning to interpret the child's reactions to past experiences from a place of compassion, understanding, and love. Love really is enough when it's given in the absence of fear. It takes seeing your child for who he is and meeting your child in his pain. It is not just meeting your child in his behavior or even at the surface of his feelings, but truly meeting your child in the depths of his fear—in the depths of his soul."

Parenting these children looks like being mindful that you are dealing with a human that has been hurt beyond imagination and approaching them with the kindness and gentleness that only God can give you. It looks like sitting with them in their pain and understanding that their behaviors are a symptom of something so much deeper. It looks like throwing choices and consequences out the window for the time being. I know that seems scary and makes zero parenting sense, but if your child is not in a place to make choices, then they aren't going to understand consequences. A child who is unable to regulate emotions or is triggered by a past event needs to have a different approach; a kind and compassionate approach that is level-headed, devoid of any strong emotion besides love.

Providing an atmosphere of "felt safety" has been key for us in seeing healing take place in our home. Just knowing they are safe isn't enough for a child at times. They need to be able to feel it. They need to be able to experience it on basic practical level in their home.

> "[P]roviding an atmosphere where your children feel and experience safety for themselves. This strategy is called providing 'felt safety.' You provide felt safety when you arrange the environment and adjust your behavior so your children can feel in a profound and basic way that they are truly safe in their home and with you. Until your child experiences safety for himself or herself, trust can't develop, and healing and learning won't progress." (*The Connected Child*)

All humans have a deeply rooted, primal need to feel safe. It's why our fight-or-flight reactions take over when we feel threatened or unsafe. "Being able to feel safe with other people is probably the single most important aspect of mental health; safe connections are fundamental to meaningful and satisfying lives." (Bessel van der Kolk, *The Body Keeps Score*) When they feel unsafe, children can become hypervigilant as they are constantly feeling like they are in danger. Racing heartbeat, shallow breathing, dilated pupils, and the inability to keep their bodies still are a few things to look out for when a child is in this state. While in this state of hypervigilance, they are constantly on alert to any dangers that may be in their surroundings. Providing an atmosphere of felt safety will go a long way to helping a child learn to trust you as the parent and learn to self-regulate in times stress.

We were able to develop a strategy of sorts when it came to parenting our children through traumatic events.

Here are some things we do or did in the Talley house.

- "Can I have your eyes?" It's so important that you try to maintain eye contact. It's the first thing I ask so I can see they are with me and not checked out completely.
- Are they hungry or thirsty? Sounds elementary, but so important that these basic needs are met before moving forward.
- Do they have felt safety? For the traumatized child, being in a safe location, even if that's your arms, is vital.
- Do they need a change of location? A ride in the car. A walk outside. Sit at the table together as they have a snack.
- Ask them what they needing from you? A hug? To just sit next to them?
- Breathe with them. Deep breaths slow the heart rate down and get blood flow back to where it needs to be so they can reason.
- Help them identify the emotion they are feeling and why. There is always a why behind behavior.
- Walk them through a redo of the situation. Show them how it can look different the next time. It sets an

expectation for them. Keep tone and volume soft as you talk. Lite, but firm. Smile. Get on their level. When they do it right, tell them!
- Walk them through cleaning up any heart messes that may have been made. "I'm sorry and I forgive you."
- Think of a quick way to connect to their heart in a positive manner. This may be the most important step. Positive connections heal the brain chemistry imbalance created by trauma. Play a card game, throw a ball, make eye contact, smile, laugh. Make a fun memory. Creating good connection memories help to override the damage done by the traumatic ones.

Dr. Karen Purvis, author of *The Connected Child*, says, "Lectures, scolding, and punishment do not help, in fact, they create even more fear. Fear must be calmed through connection and nurturing before we address behavior." I talked about connection before correction earlier in this book, but for a triggered child, this approach is paramount. Take the time to connect first so they are in a place to listen and receive. There have been times when Mike or I have tried to no avail to rationalize with our dysregulated child. No amount of logic is going to get through to that part of their brain when they are operating in survival mode. That logical, rational part of the brain has completely shut down in these moments. All they are trying to do is survive the moment.

> "We have learned that trauma is not just an event that took place sometime in the past; it is

also the imprint left by that experience on mind, brain, and body. This imprint has ongoing consequences for how the human organism manages to survive in the present. Trauma results in a fundamental reorganization of the way mind and brain manage perceptions. It changes not only how we think and what we think about, but also our very capacity to think." (*The Body Keeps Score*)

They will make absolutely no sense in their thinking because they can't access that part of the brain. We have found that connecting and working to create "felt safety" first, before we start helping them process logically through the issue, is the only way forward to conflict resolution.

Parenting the Individual

God loves us as individuals, and I feel that it's our job as parents to model that to our children. We can't have a cookie-cutter approach to parenting. There are times that we have to shift based on the individual child and what they need. We've had seasons where some of our children were craving choice and freedom and we oblige by parenting them in that way. There was a time when all I did was feel like I was talking in choices to them 24/7 or always coming up with a compromise. There have also been times when our children are craving more boundaries. Like the time my daughter asked if we could please download Life360 on our phones so we could keep track of her. We had no plans to download it for any of our children because it just didn't seem to go with our parenting style of trust, choice, and freedom, but again we obliged and got it because it made her feel safe. Then, of course, we've had seasons where we threw the current parenting style completely out the window knowing it was not what they needed in the moment.

Our Creator made us each beautifully and wonderfully as individual beings with our own personalities and interests yet made in his image. He loves us in our own unique way, purposefully and intentionally. We have our own history with God we are creating day by day as we do life with him. He knows our every wound and heartache. He knows our every victory and breakthrough. He is our biggest cheerleader and secret keeper. He loves us more than we could possibly comprehend. Most of us can read the above statement about God and say "Amen," but why don't we apply the same to our children? Why do we let adults be individuals with individual approaches to life, but not kids? Could it be that we unintentionally otherize them? I know I have been dismissive of my children. I have fallen into the old ways of "children should be seen and not heard" instead of listening to understand them. I feel with all my being that God is calling this generation of parents to a more excellent way of parenting. He's calling us to parent from a place of intentionality and compassion. He's calling us to see our children through his eyes and to guide them by the example he sets for us.

When we were blindsided some years back with a traumatic event, I remember sitting outside processing with the Lord all my pain and fear of the future. Grieving for us all and the pain we were going through. Worrying about the long, heartbreaking road we would have to walk. And then God, clear as day, said, "Jen, I have the last word on your family's life. This will not define who they are." Those words changed my whole outlook. What the enemy meant for harm God was giving a big stamp of victory. Not to say that fear never crept in again, but I almost always am able to point to that moment and remind myself God has the last word over me, my kids, my marriage. All of it. If you are a parent of a child who has experienced trauma, I see you. It is a gut-wrenchingly hard path to walk down. I know you have days where it all seems lost and hopeless. I know you weep and pour your heart out to the Lord for keys to help them through. Don't lose hope. God knows exactly what your child needs. Lean into him. He will show you the way.

• CHAPTER 5 •

Sometimes We Are Little

"I don't like frogs. They're sneaky."
—Nathan (age 4)

WE HAD LABORED FOR twelve hours through the night that ended with me delivering a 9 lb. 9 oz. baby boy via C-section. This was our start to parenthood. Exhausted, in pain, and in love with our little Nathan, we made our way home three days later. That first night he screamed all night long. Thankfully, my mom was staying with us for a bit and was able to help troubleshoot why our little guy was so unhappy. Around 3 a.m., I found Mike in the living room on the floor with his head in his hands because he felt so helpless. Sleeplessness was a major adjustment for us all. That same week Mike asked a fellow dad friend, "Does it get any better?" His friend smiled, "Ha! No, not really. You just get used to it." This one statement sort of shifted our outlook on the long road of parenting ahead. There are so many stages and ages happening in parenting. Learning to roll with them and embrace them all has been a choice we never regretted.

From the beginning, Mike and I made a conscious choice to love every stage our children went through. We didn't want to go into each age and stage predisposed to other people's views. I really think this helped us frame how we approached each age. We were excited to tackle each stage and age, from twos to twenties. We decided to be purposeful and intentional instead of dreading. I once wrote a post on Facebook about the "just waits" that we, seasoned parents, like to put on younger parents. Our intentions are always good, but leaves a negative tone for those just venturing into parenthood. Parenting is hard, but it doesn't have to be scary. You can set your mind and heart to enjoy every part.

This chapter is dedicated to the little guys. The crumb crushers. The tiny humans between the ages of one and five years old. The "I do it myself" stage. As hard and long as the days are at this age, I love it because they are all like little sponges. They soak in your every word and action. Their little personalities are developing and beginning to set in. The parts that make them an individual are starting to come out in a big way. So, how do we come alongside these little ones to teach them how to think? How do we correct them at such a young age? How do we help them learn to manage themselves even at eighteen months old? Your children are beautifully and wonderfully made. They have a beautiful mind with the ability to reason and I think they are the most underestimated age group.

Intro to Choices

When our children reached the age of around fifteen to eighteen months, we started to introduce the concept of choice. Because the world of kids this age revolves around snacks and meals, we would start to give two choices for snacks or drinks. "Do you want crackers or yogurt?" (Two choices I know they love). We would hold them up to make sure they understand the options and have them point to choose if they didn't have the words yet. When they made their choice, we would always follow with "Awesome!" or "Great choice!" Other choices we would give at this age were "Do you need help, or can you do it yourself?", "Do you want to walk, or do you want Mamma to hold you?", and "Do you want to read a book, or do you want to play with blocks?" We tried to put a choice to everything we could within reason. Introducing choice at this age is teaching them how to think, not what to think.

We would even do silly choices, just to get their brains moving as they got a little older. Especially at bedtime when crankiness would ensue. "Do you want to hop like a bunny or slither like a snake to your bedroom for bedtime?" "Do you want to brush your teeth in the bathroom or the kitchen?" Do you want to wear pajamas or sleep in your clothes?" "Do you want a bath or a shower?" "Do you want blankets or no blankets?" "Do you want your light on or off?" I can distinctly remember Mike giving the kids the choice, "Do you want to race me to the bathroom or Mom?" They all shouted "Dad!" and then he took off down our very narrow hallway with the kids thundering behind him laughing.

I'm sure you get the point. Life hinges on the ability to make wise choices. This doesn't come naturally to us as humans, it needs to be taught from a young age. The ability to reason through a problem in front of us starts with learning about choices.

Make Them Think

Right after we had made this shift in our parenting style, we were doing a big push to teach our little ones how to think. One particular time our three-and-a-half-year-old son had gotten upset and hit one of his siblings. The first thing I did was set him a chair in our kitchen called "the thinking chair." This was an idea we learned from the conference we went to. Changing the name of the designated spot from *time out chair* to *thinking chair*. The interaction went something like this:

> Me: "Charlie, do we hit or not hit?" (with a kind, quiet tone)
> Charlie: "Not hit."
> Me: "What do you think you need to do?"
> Charles: Sits for a good fifteen seconds and thinks. "You're welcome?"
> Me: "No, that's not it. You hurt your sister when you hit her. What do you think you need to do?"
> Charles: Sits and thinks for another fifteen seconds. "Thank you?"
> Me: "No, when you hit your sister, that hurt her heart. What do you think you need to do?"

Charles: Wheels turning looks at me and says, "I'm sorry?"
Me: "Yes, buddy! You need to tell Madi you are sorry and give her a hug. We are always kind with our hands."
Charles: Hops out of the chair and goes to make things right with eighteen-month-old Madi.

Parents, don't underestimate that your kids can think through what they need to do. Even as a toddler. There was no yelling or getting mad on my part. I simply asked questions. I probably would have tried one more time and then helped him remember by telling him that when we hurt someone, we say sorry. Take the time to teach them how think. Make space for that to happen. At three years old that entire interaction lasted two minutes top. I could have left him there to sit in time out by himself and he would never have gotten the chance to really think through the issue and learn from it. I never had to do that again with Charles. Did he hit again? Ha! Absolutely. I just never have to prompt him like that to apologize. The next time it happened I said, "Do we hit or not hit?" He quickly responded no and apologized on his own. Teaching children how to think is sometimes a grueling process and it seems like they will never get it, but with time and intentionality, I promise they will.

Temper Tantrums
Of course, with this age group comes the extra package of learning to manage themselves and their emotions as well. This is where the term *terrible twos* come from. My children between

the ages of two and four were in a constant learning mode of self-management from sunup to sundown. They were learning to be kind with their hands, feet, and words. They were learning to say "Sorry" and "I forgive you." They were learning just how powerful they were and that they were capable of mighty things like self-control, patience, and gentleness.

To teach them self-management when they are this young, we would of course give a choice. "Can you manage yourself, or do you need my help?" or "Can you be fun with the family, or do you need to go to your room?" If they were in a big-time fit, I might repeat the question, again asking them to look at my eyes, to get their attention. If they couldn't get themselves under wraps, then we would scoop them up and take them to their room until they calmed down. Sometimes, we'd just set them down and shut the door behind us and, other times, we'd sit in there with them depending on the kid. No time limit set. I'd just stand at their door and every minute or so I'd go in and ask, "Are you ready to be fun?" A nod and I'd scoop them back up and say something positive like, "Yay! We missed you!" or "I'm so happy you are choosing to be fun with us!" Your two-year-old is smart. It isn't going to take them long to realize they can choose to be pleasant and avoid a trip to their room. We learned "fun or room" from Danny Silk's book *Loving Our Kids on Purpose*. It is a wonderful resource for parenting children of all ages.

When they are older and these outbursts happen, there can be more of a conversation about what's going on. I would still offer the choice of managing themselves or needing my help, but a four-year-old has a way better way of communicating how they feel than a two-year-old. So, with a four- or five-year-old, I may talk to them about what caused the outburst or fit. Or I may start to introduce redos to them. Make them try again more calmly. It's helpful for resetting the expectation.

Training Days
Reflecting on those early days of parenting, I think the one thing that helped me, as a stay-at-home mom of four, was taking time to set expectations and have training days.

When Madilyn was around two years old, I started to do something called "training days" with her. Grocery shopping was beginning to become a challenge for me with a six-year-old, four-year-old, and a wide-open two-year-old cutie pie. This "I do it myself" girlie hated to have her hand held, but also hated to be pinned in the cart as well. I started to take her on trips to the store so we could practice staying by Mamma.

I would always give her a choice. "Do you want to hold Mamma's pinky, or do you want to sit in the cart?" If she couldn't manage her choice of holding my finger, then in the cart she would go for a couple of minutes. When she would calm down (yes, there were always tears), I would offer her the choice again. Of course, at two years old, neither of those choices were her favorite, but over time she learned that making the choice to hold my finger was so much more pleasant than sitting in a buggy. Honestly, giving Madilyn the choice of being able to hold my pinky and not me holding her hand made all the difference.

As we started parenting differently, we realized that some situations were still going to be stressful and having a child throw a fit in a public place ranks high on the stress scale. We found it easy to slip back into the old ways of parenting out of a place of fear. It's embarrassing to have your child lose their cool. I was always worried that others were judging me for my child's lack of self-control. I could feel the pressure to "just do something" to get them back into line. Frustration would build and I would find myself doing the exact thing I didn't want to do just to appease others. Conviction would creep in and I would end up apologizing to my two-year-old for not managing myself well. It didn't take long for me to realize that something needed to change. While my toddler didn't throw tantrums every time we went out, there were going to be times that they could not self-regulate and I might need a plan in place so I could parent out of a place of love and connection, not fear of others' opinions. Training days were a part of that plan as well as a strategy if and when those tantrums happened. If Mike was with me, one of us would remove the child from the situation, like taking them to the car until they could calm down. One of my usual go-to plans was to get them a box of animal crackers to eat as we grocery shopped and making sure they had a juice cup. Or, I would bring in a sticker book for them to play with as we did our shopping. Making sure they had a snack and a drink helped us sidestep the crankiness that can lead to behavior problems. I also avoided taking them around nap time. A tired kid is one disappointment away from a meltdown. If they threw a fit while I was by myself, I would just leave the groceries parked to the side of the entrance and walk them outside for a few minutes until they were able to manage. Then we'd try again. A plan was crucial to helping us stay on track and not revert to old parenting ways.

We taught our children to manage their freedom in the small things at a young age because we wanted them to be able to manage their freedom in the big things when they were teens and young adults. We gave them choices. We let them fail. We came alongside them and helped them learn from those fails. We let them learn from the natural consequences of life. Remember, we were created for freedom. All of us. Children just need practice in managing this amazing gift.

• CHAPTER 6 •

Sometimes We Are Big

"I wish I had a robot mom so she could play DS with me all day."
—Charles (age 8)

Whereas the previous age group is mainly focused on behavior, this elementary age group is perfect for introducing those more complex subjects. What's going on inside? Not just that you were unkind, but why were you unkind? Helping them put their emotions into words. Helping them think through the why.

For example, if my seven-year-old is unkind with their words, I might ask, "Was that honoring or dishonoring?" instead of "Do we say unkind things or not say unkind things?" I'm going to sort of harp on this subject of honor because it became such a core value in our family. All our interactions hinged on our heart posture of honor toward one another. We all learned that we could be upset and even angry about something, but we could still take ownership of ourselves in how we responded from a place of honor toward one another. We could take ownership if our actions dishonored another person in the family.

We realized that honor really had everything to do with us and how we modeled it for our children. We couldn't require honor if we didn't know how to show it to our kids. To us, honor looked like watching our tone, being kind, saying sorry (biggie), listening to them, giving them a voice (another biggie), and creating a safe place to fail. Honor flows from the top down. Honor is self-sacrifice and serving one another.

Charlie's Choice

Let's talk a minute about big kid choices. These choices look a bit different from those of a younger kid. We used them just as consistently, but we let them learn more from the natural consequences of life. For example, if I've asked my children to put shoes on before they go outside and they forget or just choose not to, then I can sit back and watch the learning happen. Usually in the form of feet getting hurt or the pavement top being a little too hot on their toes. Natural consequences, to me, are better than any argument or power struggle that I might have with my child. I can tell my child what will happen if they don't wear shoes, but some kids, like mine, really like to experience life for themselves. No amount of Mom's warning is going to change their mind, but a walk on some hot pavement might. We used these moments to let them experience the pain of poor choices.

A real-life example of this for our family was what we like to refer to as the "hose story." Bedtime with a nine-, seven-, five-, and two-year-old was always quite an ordeal at our house. We had a pretty good routine down with baths, stories, cuddles, and finally sleep. We would usually pull out the silly choices if there was crankiness or overtired kids to deal with; and, on this particular night, our second born, Charles, was struggling with getting in the shower.

> Mike: "Hey, buddy, time for your shower!"
> Charles: Whining. "I don't want to get a shower."
> Mike: "I know you don't, but it's almost bedtime and you need to make sure you are all clean before you hop in bed."
> Charles: Still digging in and whiny, "I don't like showers."
> Mike: "Would you like to take a shower inside, or outside with the hose?"
> (Keep in mind, it was fall and a bit chilly outside.)
> Charles: "I can do that?"
> Mike: "You sure can! Would you like to take a shower inside or clean up outside with the hose?"
> Charles: "Outside!"
> Mike: Grabbed the shampoo, soap, and a towel and said, "Let's go!"

I watched from the window as Mike hosed him down and Charles was increasingly looking colder and colder as the seconds clicked by. Charles hadn't factored in that hose water is quite chilly compared to shower water.

He came in shivering saying, "The hose was so cold!" We just agreed with him, told him to get his pj's on, and off to bed he went. The next night, when bedtime routine rolled around, you better bet that Charles had zero issues taking his shower inside. Ha! We still laugh about what a great learning experience that was for Charles. Let them learn in a safe place. Failing equals learning for the next time they are faced with the same problem.

Mei's Third Choice
Sometimes, some of our stronger-willed kids like to come up with a third choice outside the parameters of the choices we gave them. These third choices are not a bad thing in and of themself, but there are times that the choice they give isn't going to work in the situation we are in. In these cases, we usually repeat the two we've given and then say, "You choose or I choose," giving them the signal that these are the only two choices they get and, if they can't choose between these two, then we will be happy to choose for them. I can promise you most kids are not going to want you to choose for them. I personally don't mind my children picking a third choice, especially if it's going to bring about a perfect learning experience.

Our daughter, Mei, was notorious for offering a third choice. She never liked to feel confined to just two. One such time was when she was around seven or eight years old, she wanted to ride a teacup-type ride at a local amusement park.

Knowing how motion sick she would get, I explained I didn't think that would be a good idea and gave her two other ride choices to choose. She promptly stated, "I want to ride the teacups and I want to ride it myself." I told her I didn't think that was a great idea and gave her the choice of the other two rides again to no avail. So, on the teacup ride she went all by herself. I remember watching her get on that ride all by herself in that big ole teacup. The ride started out slow, but Mei soon realized that she indeed didn't like these type of rides. Round and round she went. By the time she got off, she was so green and spent the next two hours throwing up. I never had to tell her "I told you so." I never got on to her. I just told her I was sorry she was sick and helped her navigate the consequence of her choice. She is now fifteen years old and can remember that day so vividly. The ride, the spinning, the laying down in the wagon feeling so sick. She asked me why I let her do it. I told her sometimes that third choice created a great time for learning, and she learned that day to next time maybe stick to the two choices at hand and trust Mom. Maybe the next time she would think through the choice she was trying to make.

Creating a Space to Fail
Failures are a part of life and we tried to make our home a place where it was safe to fail. With emphasis on the word TRY, we had lots of parenting fails in this area, mostly from parenting out of our pain. When thinking of examples of how we did or didn't make our home a safe place, two stories popped in my head. The first is a parent fail on our part of what not to do

when children make mistakes. Sadly, it is the opposite of how we wanted to create a safe place for our children to be human.

Practice kid number 1 took the brunt of our learning curve unfortunately. When we started this new parenting path, he was already five years old. He is able to remember the before, after, and all the mistakes we made in trying to shift. I'm pretty sure he's heard "I'm sorry" from us more than any of the others. When he was around eight years old, he had a Nintendo DS that was his favorite toy. With a family of four, he was at the top of three younger siblings whose ages at that time were six, four, and one.

One day, his four-year-old sibling got ahold of it and broke it. Sadly, our immediate reaction was to fuss at him for letting his little sister get ahold of it. We didn't come alongside him and have compassion or empathy for his loss. Our fear of raising an irresponsible child won over and we shamed him into thinking that he could have prevented a four-year-old from getting ahold of his stuff. This one act on our part caused him to make an inner vow that he would guard his toys and not let anyone touch them. We started to see this sweet, kind, and generous little boy become guarded and hard when it came to sharing. It wasn't until years later that the Lord told Mike and I that we needed to apologize to him. We wrote him a letter one Christmas morning when he was twelve years old apologizing for hurting him and coming down too hard on him. As he read we saw tears falling and we knew that this had been such a deep hurt for him and now healing was taking place. It broke our hearts to know our actions were the cause of such hurt.

Unfortunately, this wasn't a one-time incident. We have failed our children more that I can count. We have reacted poorly or let our own issues get in the way of showing the Father's heart, but just like with our children, our failures help us learn going forward. We have learned that there is no shame in apologizing. If anything, it has helped our children see us as human, just like them. So many times I have had to humble myself in front of my children and own the hurt I have caused them. Failures go both ways in the parent–child relationship.

Creating a safe place to fail meant that we needed to prioritize connection over correction. When our thirteen-year-old left their iPhone in the pocket of their jeans on laundry day, we were all devastated. Having an iPhone was a long-awaited privilege in our family and this mistake was costly. Mike and I didn't fuss or yell or lecture on irresponsibility. We simply put our arms around them and told them we were so sorry. When they asked if they could get a new one, we explained that our finances could not afford us to buy a new one at the moment. Tears were shed as we walked them through processing their disappointment. About six months later, a new iPhone was given and a new sense of responsibility was instilled as they guarded that phone with their life. The stark difference in these two stories is that our parenting actions caused a disconnect in one and maintained connection in the other. One was from a place of fear, the other from a place of empathy and love.

As we moved through the parenting years, we found that being intentional about how we dealt with failures was helpful. One way we did this was that we instituted a rule that made it safe to tell the truth. Mike and I had multiple conversations with all our children that gave them permission to tell the truth with no harsh repercussions. Children lie when they feel like they are about to get in trouble or they feel cornered. We always celebrated truth even if they were in the wrong in their actions. Addressing the behavior came second to rejoicing in the truth first. Telling the truth is often an act of bravery for children and we wanted our kids to always feel they could come to us with any problem. Creating that space built a level of trust between us and the children that has carried us through the hard parts of growing up when they are teens. We attempted to create a nonreactive space to their mistakes.

> "I'm so sorry you left your toy at Aunt Mimi's. I bet your miss it so much."
>
> "I know you are sad about missing Boy Scouts because you have to mow the lawn. Do you need help managing your time?"
>
> "I know you don't like to sit in the buggy and that makes me sad too. Would you like to try to hold my hand now?"
>
> "Oh, man, it's so sad when we have to sit in the thinking chair. Do we hit or not hit?"
>
> "I know you are so cold from taking a shower with the hose. What do you think you need to do next time?"

"I'm so sorry you hurt your foot running around outside. Would you like me to help you put your shoes on?"

Coming alongside our kids in their time of failure to encourage not condemn has helped make our home a safe space to make messes. Just this week, one of my teens had come to me with a problem she was having in self-management, and I just sat there and listened as she teared up asking for my help in a particular area of struggle. I told her I love her and was happy to help keep her accountable, that I'm sorry it's been such a struggle and that she was fully capable of kicking this issue to the curb. At some point, she looked at me and said, "Thank you for being such a good mom and not bringing down the hammer on me. It makes me feel that I can come to you with anything." This. This level of trust didn't come overnight. If you put the work in when they are young, creating a history of trust, it will pay in dividends when they are teens and start having adult issues to combat. To be clear, this doesn't mean that we just let them run into oncoming traffic or put themselves in a life-threatening situation. There are times where our voice needs to be paramount. Boundaries are important and necessary for the safety of children. To me, this is where a history of trust helps in the parent–child relationship. If I've built a relationship of kindness, gentleness, and honor, then the likelihood that my child will pause at the sound of my voice will be high.

• CHAPTER 7 •

Sometimes We Have Hormones

"Are you sure you got my birthday right?"
—Nathan (age 12)

WORDS THAT COME TO mind when I think of these middle grade years: *weepy, hormonal, body changing, weepy, funny, gross humor, mood swings, weepy.* They are upside down, hormonal preteens and teens. I have so much grace for them though and it may be one of my favorite ages to date. I remember these being the years that they finally started getting my sarcastic jokes. They also thought I was still pretty cool in sixth grade until they entered seventh grade and then I was very uncool. This is also the age where they really were trying to figure themselves out as individuals. They started to care what they wore and how their hair looked. Started looking to celebrities they liked as a styling guide. Taking a bath was no longer a chore. Hormone surges brought tears and frustration. Although choices were still given and lots of learning was always happening, they were starting to think more abstract. By seventh or eighth grade they started to ask the hard questions about life, and we did our best to help them start to form their own worldview of things. We never wanted them to regurgitate our thoughts on hard issues. We pointed them to truth, yet always gave them permission to disagree with us.

I asked my kids recently if they could think of any memories or stories that happened during those years. I already had one in mind, but for the life of me I couldn't remember any others. My daughters told me the only thing they remember is lots of crying, awkwardness, and long conversations with Mom. It made me laugh because that pretty much sums up all their experiences during those years. I felt like we would just grab hands in sixth grade and pray them through to the other side of ninth or tenth grade. Honestly, I remember lots of grace and understanding being given at this age. Especially with emotions going all over the place. I can remember my oldest standing in his room one afternoon at twelve years old. Puberty came early for him, so his twelve-year-old body had a man's voice coming out of it. He was sobbing asking if we had gotten his birthday correct. He was so out of sorts with his growing and changing that he had started to question his birth certificate. Bless him.

Life with my kids was a roller coaster of emotions during these years. So much learning going on, especially from me. There is so much growing up between the ages of ten and sixteen. Growing pains are real, especially the ones of the heart and mind. Mentally shifting with their ever-changing world was a challenge for me sometimes, but necessary for us all to stay in connection with one another. I had to learn to shift with them. The number of times they needed me to hold their hand in situations started to decrease. I found myself feeling like a fish out of water at times as I reached to take a hand that no longer needed mine. It took me a few times to realize they needed me to walk beside them not lead them anymore. They still wanted me close beside them, but they didn't need me to take the reins all the time. Instead of assuming they wanted my opinion, I started to ask questions like, "Would you like my feedback on that?" or "I have some thoughts. Would you like to hear them?" I started to listen more than I spoke. I started to let go more and more so they could have the freedom to make choices and decisions for themselves.

Mohawk Story
"Hey, Mom, I want to get a Mohawk."

This was coming from the same kid who would want me to use my hair straightener on his longer hair to make it look like Justin Bieber. A Mohawk?!

My first reaction was, "What will people think?" We were associate pastors of a church at the time and it felt like all eyes were on us and our children with our every move being watched. We had worked hard on creating a culture of freedom in our home and this felt like a test of my fortitude. My second reaction was, "What if he hates it?" He was going to have to live with this choice for quite a while if he didn't like it. I understood the social dynamics of middle school age and I was worried he may regret this choice big time.

Then the Holy Spirit whispered. "It's just hair."

I had a choice in that moment. I could trust the years of giving choices and making them think or I could start trying to discourage him from expressing himself. I mean, the kiddo had confidence to just come out and tell me what he wanted. Ha! He didn't extend an invitation to this decision by asking my thoughts. He simply made a statement. "Mom, I want to get a Mohawk." Not "Mom, can I get a Mohawk?" or "Mom, what do you think about me getting a Mohawk?" It was the first time I wasn't invited to this decision-making party. He had thought it through to the best he could at thirteen years old and had made his choice.

My response (deep breath), "Wow! I think that's a great idea! Do you want to look up pictures on my phone to show the barber?" (exhale) And he did. He looked at pictures and found the perfect one and off to the barber we went.

He looked so good. He took a risk. It was a huge decision for him. A decision he made on his own. I asked Nate today what his perspective was of the whole thing. He is twenty-two and married now. He said he remembered being into the Call of Duty video game and the main character had one and he said, "I want that." He said at first he regretted it because he was afraid that others might judge him, but everyone said it was cool so he felt better. When I asked him if he was shocked we let him get one, or that we didn't give him a hard time, he said and I quote, "Nope." Man of few words.

Scary Freedom

At the age of thirteen, we gifted each of the kids their first iPhone. With intentionality in mind, we always made a big deal of how much freedom they were being given. Mike had an iPhone speech that he gave to each of our four children on their thirteenth birthday. It went something like this:

"I am handing you a tremendous amount of freedom. I am nervous and scared that you are not going to manage this very well. Can you take care of my heart with this freedom I am giving you?"

As we all know, as much fun as there is to be had with an iPhone (games, music, etc.) there are also a bunch of not-so-fun things that can be accessed on an iPhone (nudity, porn, bullying, stranger danger, etc.). We knew there would be challenges so we asked each of them to come to us if they were struggling with things their eyes were seeing so we could help them, not punish them. We did regular phone checks, had rules surrounding the use of iPhones at certain times of the day, and had other basic safeguards, but that doesn't mean our kids didn't stumble across inappropriate images or find themselves looking at things they shouldn't be looking at. On more than one occasion we have had our children come to us for help in this department. Keeping connection in mind, these conversations went something like this:

"Thank you for being honest. It took a lot of courage for you to come to me. This isn't what you should be using your iPhone for though and it's not honoring to women or men when we look at these images. What do you think you need to do about this?"

Most of the time the kids would suggest deleting the app that was causing issues for a while. We would tell them to pray and ask the Lord for when he thinks they would be able to handle the app again. When they felt they were ready to handle it, they would come back to us and we'd talk it over and install the app back on their phone. One of our children deleted an app for an entire six months until they felt ready.

Keeping this open communication showed them that nothing was off the table as far as questions or confessions they had for us. The topics ran the gamut of porn, drugs and alcohol, abortion, objectifying women and men, choosing friends wisely, or even politics. This is the age they are desperately trying so hard to find their voice. They want to be a part of the conversation. So much of our time during these years was just spent listening to them. Not really offering advice besides the occasional feedback on friendships or relationships. It was spent more on listening to understand. Trying to hear with our heart all the emotions and feelings that they were experiencing. When my youngest daughter started to ask questions about her birth parents, we had to learn to be OK with not having all the answers and to trust that the Lord would give us the words to help her navigate through the grief and sorrow of abandonment. When another teen was experiencing anxiety over friendships, we would listen, pray, and point them to the only one who could help them through. I'm pretty sure it was during these years that each kid heard the words, "I am not your savior. I never will be. I will fail you. Only Jesus has all the answers" or "What does Jesus say about that? Have you asked him?" Keeping connection was paramount, but so was fostering their relationship with Jesus by teaching them to take everything to him. So many times, I had this conversation with each one of my kids. I could not and still cannot be their everything. I think that's what I learned most from those years. I learned to listen to understand and release them to the one who loved them more than I did. I learned to trust that he would hold their hand when they didn't need me to anymore.

Prayer

These hard conversations brought about the amazing opportunity to teach our children about the power of prayer. When they were small, we would say bedtime prayers, having them repeat after us. There is nothing more precious than a toddler saying "God bless" prayers at bedtime. Never forgetting to leave anyone out in the entire family, these could drag on for a bit, but it was foundational to their future relationship with God. As they got older, we started to use an inner healing tool used to connect people to the Godhead. We called it "finding Jesus." God gave us our minds and imaginations and this tool helped our children to create a mental picture of Jesus that they could connect to when praying. If any of them were struggling and hurt or had a hard decision to make, we would tell them to find Jesus and then guide them through asking Jesus those hard questions and then listening to the truth he spoke to them. A little unconventional, I know, but it really helped though the years as they built their own history with

God. They all had their own versions of what Jesus looked like. One of my daughters still sees him as a big lion, like Aslan from *The Chronicles of Narnia*. Another sees him as a bright light. They all had their special places he would take them. A mountain stream on a park bench or relaxing in a hammock. So many sweet and difficult conversations between them and Jesus. I would just sit there in awe as I watched Jesus calm their fears and speak words of truth to them. He knew them better than me. He loved them more than me. He knew exactly what they needed to hear. As the years went on, we got front row seats to their relationship with God.

Our oldest daughter Madilyn had a speech impediment when she was younger in that she could not say her *r*'s. Although this was cute when she was younger, she began to get self-conscious of it as she got older. We looked into speech therapy, but at every turn God would close doors. At the same time this was going on, Madilyn also was tormented by a spirit of fear that started to creep into every part of her life. At one point she was so scared of getting sick from germs that she refused to open her mouth to speak. Every night she would ask the Lord to help her *r*'s and take the spirit of fear away from her.

When she was thirteen years old, she went off to a youth retreat where she had a radical encounter with Jesus and was delivered from a spirit of fear! She was so excited when she came home and told us. The next Sunday she boldly led worship for everyone at church on Youth Sunday no fear in sight. My very favorite part of this story is that the very next morning when she woke up, she came to tell me good morning and every bit of her speech impediment was gone. Not a trace of it was left. Only God! I love this testimony because Mike and I had nothing to do with it. We couldn't take her fear away and we definitely could not correct her speech. Madilyn will never forget that God came through for her in a supernatural way. It's a part of her history with the Lord.

Charles struggled with sleep at a young age and would have nightmares nightly for a while. Mike would sit in a chair in his room reading the Bible and praying over him as he fell asleep. The Lord gave us Psalm 91 to read over him nightly and Charles would say it with us. He eventually had the entire chapter memorized and would pray it over himself. The nightmares ceased and sleep came easier. He did this for years.

God wants a relationship with our children. He sees them as individuals and loves them so much more than we can fathom. Letting our children contend for themselves and see the breakthrough that happens has not only built their faith, but ours as well. As teens and young adults, they now come to us and ask us to partner with them in prayer over certain things. It's been so much fun to watch them from the sidelines as the Lord comes through for them time after time.

There is power in remembering the goodness of God. When trials come, and they will because Jesus said they would, we have to have something to hold on to. We need to have a history of how God broke through for us so we can stand in faith that he is good. Our children need the same thing. At some point they need their own memories of how God turned his face towards them and let his favor shine on them. These years full of hormones and mood swings are the perfect age to start letting them see God work all things out for them. At an age when the world seems to be against them, they need something to hold onto. They need to experience God in a very real way, so they won't depart form him when things get tough. The years that follow go by in a blink as they rapidly approach adulthood. The issues at hand are more mature and costly. The falls can be hard. The lessons can be tough. They will need their relationship with the Lord to be strong as they navigate through.

• CHAPTER 8 •

Sometimes We Fall in Love

"Well, when he sees me in my princess dress, he will know I love him."
—Madilyn (age 7 talking about getting married)

I FEEL LIKE THIS chapter has been such a challenge for me to write. How do you write about something you are currently walking through? I feel confident in my approach to the other chapters because we are through those ages and can say what worked or didn't work with some assurance; but we happen to be smack in the middle of this dating season with our kids, so I wanted to take a second and preface that this chapter is currently a work in progress, as we live it out in real time. Mike and I have some core values that we instill at this age of teenagerhood, but as we learn daily, our children may or may not choose to hold onto them as tightly as we do. This beautiful age of fifteen to twenty years old is a growth spurt of learning and clinging to their own ideals. They are forming or have already formed opinions about the world around them. We are reminded that connection is key, not to make sure they think like us, but to make sure that as they move forward in life, they always know they are loved, even if they make choices we don't agree with.

The scary part of letting our children live in a culture of freedom is that one day they may choose to do things differently than us or they may choose a path that leads down a long, sad road. There is absolutely no guarantee that our parenting, and raising them to know who their Savior is, will keep them safe or from painful choices. There is no cookie-cutter formula to parenting that will prevent them from choosing to walk down scary roads in life. The only thing we can do, as parents, is to point them to the only one who loves them more than we do. If they find themselves lost, they know in their knower that they are loved beyond measure by Jesus and can come to him with anything. Also, we trust that our connection to them, built over years, will mean that they know they can come to us as well. All parents want their children to make the right choices, but the reality is that at some point they may not and that's the hard part.

With that said, the following chapter is for the teenage dating ages. There are a lot of subjects we could cover with these ages, but we've decided to home in on just one of those possible problematic issues in the area of dating. Our experience has been far from perfect in this area and our goal is not to expose our children in any way. That's not the point or heart of this chapter. Our heart is to show how we currently are navigating through this season with our children. The standard of protecting purity is high in our house. It's our desire to help them guard that part of their life as they delve into these relationships.

Navigating the world of dating with our kids has added a whole new chapter to our parenting journey. We currently have three out of the four children either married or in a serious relationship. Two of those dating currently (ages eighteen and twenty) are still living at home with us, as well as our youngest. Needless to say, we are in the throes of this stage of parenting.

Six years into this part of raising our children and I think we've decided that dating can be a good thing if intentionality is at the core. Mike reminded me that we sort of started with this idea when the kids were little. We made a point to not tease them about having a girlfriend or boyfriend when they were young. If our boys had a friend that was a girl, we never made a big deal about it and the same went for the girls. I think we never wanted to cheapen the idea of an opposite sex relationship or even make it seem silly. All relationships are treasures and, when the time came for those boy/girl relationships, we wanted them to take these seriously. There were several things we encouraged through these dating years. We always encouraged friendship first, not dating anyone they wouldn't consider a relationship with, and, finally, not wasting their time or yours if they feel like it's not going to lead to marriage.

Just Be Their Friend
This is all we ever tell our children if they are starting to show interest in another. Just start at the beginning. Be a friend. Start with getting this down first. If the relationship has any chance of moving forward in a healthy manner, then friendship must be the foundation. We have shared with them that there have been times in our marriage when life got hard and all we had to hold onto was that friendship. All we could do was love each other out of that friend heart. You can't date someone intentionally and not be friends. The friendship build up is different for everyone though. My oldest and his wife were friends at twelve years old and didn't start dating until sixteen years old. They had 4 years of friendship before they even thought about moving it forward. My daughter and her now boyfriend were friends for only five months before they decided to move their relationship to dating. The point is that no matter the length we always encouraged being friends first.

At some point, when things are looking like something deeper is developing, we start to ask questions like, "Is this someone you could consider a future with? Is this someone who you think you'd want to marry one day?" Some may think that this is just way too heavy for any teen to even have to consider, but I think that if you've taught your kids the value of relationships then they can handle these things. If they can't answer or feel overwhelmed by the thought of thinking of a future with this person, then they aren't ready to date responsibly. There is another person's heart on the other end of this friendship they have, and that heart needs to be considered before jumping into a romantic relationship. We wanted our kids to understand the weight of the responsibility of this next step.

Just because they could consider a future with this person does not mean they are stuck in this relationship. We haven't had this happen yet, but, if for some reason the relationship wasn't what they thought or if the Lord wasn't in it, then I know we would encourage them to love the other enough to bring the relationship back to friendship only. There is no reason to continue in something that is no longer going to end in marriage. It would be wasting their time as well as the other person's.

Our experience in this area has been smoother than anticipated, if not atypical. So far, our oldest son had his first girlfriend at the age of sixteen and married her at eighteen (almost nineteen). Our oldest daughter had her first boyfriend at seventeen and now, one year into their relationship, they both are working toward an end goal of marriage within this year. Charles and Emily started dating at the age of twenty. Both had set their minds on relationships from the start. If you ask any of them, they will say they knew early on that this was their forever person. Aryanna, Nathan's wife, says she knew at the age of twelve, when she first met Nate, that she has never been surer of anything in her life. She knew four whole years before Nathan asked her out. Jared knew before he and Madilyn started dating. The Lord sealed that in his heart when they were just in the friendship stage of things. Charles says he knew a couple of months into their relationship that he wanted Emily to be his forever person. The one thing that all of them had in common was that none of them wanted to date just for the sake of dating. They all wanted to date on purpose and intentionally with the end goal of relationship. None of them wanted to waste time. None of them were waiting for the perfect person. Those people do not exist. They simply learned to love the person that God put in front of them, faults and all. We remind them that the only person they can change or work on in this relationship is themselves. I know this may not be the norm for everyone. I sometimes feel that our experience in this may be the exception to the rule. I fully expected all my children to do as Mike and I did and date more than one person, but so far that hasn't been our experience Although, we do have one more to go with the baby of the family currently at almost age sixteen. This area of friendship has been vital to all our children as they started dating. I asked them if I could briefly share their stories just so I could give some context as to how it looked for us.

Nate and Aryanna's Story
In the spring of 2016, when Nathan and Aryanna were fifteen years old, Aryanna approached Nathan about taking their friendship to the next step of dating. Nate came to Mike asking for his advice on the situation and expressed that he didn't feel that he was ready for a relationship and didn't want to lose Aryanna as a friend. He told Ary that he just wanted to remain friends. Mike knew that this would be devastating to Ary, so he encouraged Nate to keep up the friendship with her through

the summer. It took a while, but they eventually started texting again and, in August of that same year, Aryanna decided to go out on a limb and invited Nate to a homecoming game at her high school. What a difference five months made for Nathan! He was ready for a relationship this time and a couple of weeks later asked her out on their first date. They have been married for three-and-a-half years now. I love this story because Nathan wanted to be careful not to step into something he wasn't emotionally ready to handle. As risky as it was that he may have lost her as a friend, he knew he couldn't put her or his heart on the line by stepping into something he couldn't handle. To this day, the family teases Nate for friend-zoning his future wife, but what a difference it made in their ability to move forward intentionally.

Madilyn and Jared's Story
Madilyn and Jared met in spring of 2021 at a youth group. Madilyn was sixteen at the time. Both were asked to help lead youth worship at church and formed a friendship after months of having to work together. Madilyn was new to the group and every Wednesday she would come home and I'd ask, "Who did you talk to tonight?" and time after time she would say, "Just Jared." They soon became inseparable in their friendship and, as they grew closer over the summer and through the fall of that year, Madilyn realized her feelings were growing stronger toward Jared. She finally worked up the nerve to talk to him about it and they decided to shift their friendship toward a relationship. They have been dating a year now.

Charles and Emily's Story

Early in 2022, Charles (twenty years old) came to me and told me he had started praying for God to bring him a girlfriend and he asked me to partner with him in this. I happily did and, in June of the same year, he asked to talk to Mike and I and told us that he had created a profile for himself on a couple of online dating apps. He went on to say that he had connected with a girl from a neighboring town, and he had been talking to her for a couple of weeks. Her name was Emily and he needed advice about what to do for a first date. By late July, they had decided to make it official and start dating. As we were laughing about this bizarre story the other evening, Charles said, "It shouldn't have worked, but here we are six months later!" They had a small window of friendship compared to the others, but those six weeks or so laid a foundation for them to move forward.

Friendship plays such a vital role in our relationships. Each one of our children's experiences in this has been completely different from one another, but friendship has been at the core of each of them. Friendship is where we learn if the other is trustworthy and safe to share our thoughts with. It's a sweet time of getting to know the other without the pressures that come with taking the next step into committed relationship. It's not a stage to be skipped over or shoved aside as a waste of time, especially for a young person just trying to figure it all out. Starting here lays a foundation for any movement forward in the future.

Sex

Can't write a chapter on dating and not talk about sex. Sorry. I know for some this may feel uncomfortable, but we as Christians have got to get over ourselves in this area. God created sex. He created sex and he just like everything he created he said it was good. I don't know where it all went sideways for us as believers to skirt this subject, but I think it's doing our young people a huge disservice to avoid the subject. With that said, Mike and I decided to not shy away from the subject with the kids. We were very purposeful in taking the time when they were mature enough to explain what sex is to them. He talked to the boys, and I talked to the girls. The first sex conversation was simply explaining body parts, how they worked, what sex was, and it ended with that God made it and it was a good thing. As they got older, we'd talk about how and why God made sex to stay within the confines of marriage. When they started dating, we talked about how waiting until marriage was something they were going to have to fight for. That it would not be easy, but it would be worth it.

Mike would tell the boys, "Trust me, I didn't wait and I regret that more than you will ever know. God made sex to be part of marriage so that afterwards you feel no shame or fear. Sex outside of marriage produces all of these." In this instant gratification society, this is becoming increasingly difficult for kids to grasp much less manage. Delaying gratification is so foreign to people. Setting a core value of waiting until married is rare, even in Christian circles. It needs to be taught in the home and in churches, but it can't be taught if we are afraid to even broach the subject. Our kids deserve so much better. I can't stress enough to be bold in helping your children in the area of sex. Explain in plain language, be there to answer any and all uncomfortable questions, and come alongside them if mistakes are made. It doesn't have to be scary or controlling. In the end, the responsibility to protect themselves and each other in this area rests on their shoulders, but we can make sex less taboo by just being open and honest with our kids. One of the ways that Mike and I have tackled this subject is to be vulnerable with our teens about our dating days. We were far from perfect and we let them know it. We let them know that we understand the difficulties of making it until marriage. We tell them that we made poor choices that led us down a road to not being able to make it. Mike and I tell them the regrets we had and that the Lord convicted us later in marriage and we had to repent. We explain that we didn't have nor did we ever even think to set boundaries for ourselves in this area. Remaining honest about our failures, yet still encouraging purity has made for some awkward conversations, but we had to settle that it's OK for our children to see us in a different light. It opened a door for them to know they could come to us with any and all questions they might have.

Boundaries

Boundaries are so important when dating starts. If they are teens when they start dating, we have set some house rules that we ask to be followed until they are at a place relationally to set their own boundaries. Our house rules consist of taking a sibling along for dates, not being alone in cars or rooms, and lots of hanging out with the family. We've also learned that opening our home for hanging out and just doing life has been a game changer. It has served a dual purpose of getting to know the new significant other as well as them getting to know us. Family card games have been a fun way for us all to connect. It was a more engaging time than just sitting and watching a movie and less intimidating than forced conversation around the dinner table. We include them in family celebrations like birthdays, holidays, and even family vacations. We want them to feel safe to be themselves as well as feel that they have a place in our family and, no matter how long or short, that they are part of our life.

Once the relationship is a little more established and we feel the timing is ready, we loosen up the house rules and boundaries and encourage them to make their own. It's important that they start to take ownership of their choices and actions with one another. Our son, Nate, and his then girlfriend, Aryanna, each made a separate list of boundaries that they wanted in place. We call this a "how we aren't going to have sex until married" plan. They were sixteen at the time and were encouraged to get as detailed as possible in their individual plans. This is where we refused to shy away from the uncomfortable topics of sex. We cannot expect our children to be successful in their goals without a plan in place. So, as awkward as it might be, I will always encourage making a plan and doing their best to follow their purity plan. I asked them If I could share the main parts of their purity plan that helped them.

Nathan and Aryanna's Purity Plan:

1. Someone has to be in the house with us
2. No closed doors
3. If you have to be alone, tell someone where you're going and how long
4. Try not to sit alone in a car for too long (usually we would stand outside of the car if it was too hot)
5. Have people you trust check up on you
6. Tell the other person if you feel like you're struggling with a specific situation

Madilyn and Jared and Charles and Emily, although a little older when they started dating, were encouraged to do the same thing. We are all human and we don't expect perfection. I think it would be highly unfair to put that on any of my teens, but we do expect repentance and heart changes. We come alongside them and remind them of the goal ahead and we also remind them that crossing boundary lines is getting closer to taking something that isn't theirs to take. That privilege belongs to their future spouse and, while I hope it will one day be each other, the fact is that until they are married, they have zero business dancing around that boundary line.

Freedom Can Be Scary
So, what happens if our kids cross this boundary and have sex before they get married? What if they disagree with us that there is anything wrong with it? In this culture of freedom we have created, we know that it is highly possible that one or all

of our children may choose to have sex before they get married. There are several factors that would go into our response to them, but the most important one being that their behavior would not affect our ability to approach the situation with love and gentleness. Just as when they were small, my job is to maintain connection first and correction second. Other than making sure that our hearts were poised toward them with love, I think the rest of our response would depend on their age. A fifteen- or seventeen-year-old choosing to have sex is a different ballgame than an eighteen- or twenty-year-old choosing to have sex. The most obvious difference being one is still considered a teen and the other considered an adult, but also the mental and emotional maturity between fifteen and twenty is massive. I cannot control what my young teen does outside my home without my presence, but I can set parameters around when, where, and with whom our sixteen-year-old dates. Time limits and chaperones would probably be set in place. Here is the simple truth, if they really want to have sex, they will find places to do it, but I can make their world a bit smaller to be able to do those things. We would ask the hard questions about their relationship with God because, at that point, it's a heart issue between them and God. For an older teen or adult living in our house who has chosen to have sex before marriage, we would let them know that we do not agree with this choice they are making and that while we cannot control their choices outside our home, we can put some parameters in place while they live at home. Clear boundaries as to what can and cannot happen in our home would be talked about. We would maintain a heart posture of love while at the same time expressing our heart of disappointment and concern. We would most definitely ask about their relationship with the Lord. When any sin issue comes into play, whether it be lust or jealousy or anything else, there is a disconnect between them and God. If we did not see a heart change, then we would probably encourage them that it is time to move on out of the house. Not as punishment, but from a place of "It's time for you to stand on your own two feet because, obviously, you are wanting to make adult decisions." Adult children at some point do not need to answer to us, they need to answer to the Lord. Their decisions are between them and God. As Mom and Dad, we can give our input, but we have to let them grow up and make those decisions that we may not agree with. If these adult decisions are impacting the family at home, then as parents we will take steps to protect the home. If our adult children are on their own and make these choices then, as stated, that is between them and the Lord. We still would maintain our heart posture of love towards them.

The goal of maintaining one's purity before marriage is a challenging one. Is it attainable? Yes. Will they choose to always have self-control in this area? My hope is that they will, but the reality is they may not. Mike and I have had to settle that some of our children may decide that this standard is too impossible to maintain. Relationships are hard. Staying a virgin while dating the love of your life is hard. Making plans and keeping boundaries is hard. Our connection to them is key to helping them through no matter what choices are made. They don't need us to make it any more difficult for them by bringing down the hammer if mistakes are made. They need to know that Mom and Dad are safe for them to come to when they screw up. They need to know that we are here to champion them on and help them be successful in every part of their life.

Encouragement to Parents

Parents, we can do everything right, but in the end our children will grow up and make their own choices. We can take them to church, bathe them in scripture, and immerse them in all things Jesus and they still have the ability to walk away. I saw an Instagram post that reminded us parents that Jesus, the most perfect teacher, even had a close disciple walk away from him. Pray for them. Place them in the Lord's hands. It's possible you may feel like a failure after having put all of the years of work and sacrifice into your child only to have them walk away or walk down a path of destruction. I know your heart may be breaking over their choices, but let me remind you that God promises that our children will not depart from his teachings. (Proverbs 22:6) He is a relentless God who never ever gives up on his children. He will always be standing on the porch waiting for them to come home. So keep your eyes on the horizon. Pray for the Lord to capture their hearts. They will make their way back.

• CHAPTER 9 •

Sometimes We Need to Say Sorry

"I'm going to do what's best for me even if it hurts my feelings."
—Mei (age 14)

SAYING SORRY HAS BECOME a necessary action in our home in order to maintain relationships with one another. We taught it from an early age that when you've wronged someone, you say "I'm sorry." We always encouraged the kids to keep short accounts with one another. In other words, don't let an offense fester. Just communicate your heart quickly so the other person can own their part in it or maybe explain their heart back. As we got on in our years of parenting, I came to realize that this actually had become a discipline of some sorts to the kids. It became their normal to communicate hurts, apologize, and forgive quickly. When the kids started dating, this was probably one of the biggest adjustments that their significant others had to deal with. Just the other night we were all around the table and someone said something about being hurt. I said,

"Yeah, if anything, the Talleys know how to communicate hurt feelings." Madilyn's boyfriend's eyes got really big and he said, "Yes, they do!" Teaching our children to be intentional with one another's hearts was just as important as teaching them to manage their choices. With honor at the helm, mess ups and clean ups became an everyday way of life.

Cleaning Up Messes
We learned the phrase *"cleaning up messes"* from the speaker and author Danny Silk. He likened hurting other people with our words and actions to someone dropping a can of paint in a room. Who got splattered by the paint? Who got messy because of your actions? Those are the hearts you need to clean up. When they were little, we started using the *"clean up our mess"* phrase often. "Oh, no! You made a mess when you said that to your brother. What do you think you need to do to clean up that mess?"

Sometimes it was several people who got hit with the mess. "Is there anyone else who got their heart hurt? Do you need my help remembering?" I think the point we were trying to convey was that life is messy. We can hurt others with our actions and words, even unintentionally, and it's our job to take ownership of our words and actions when we hurt people. This last little bit here is probably the most important lesson we taught our kids. We taught them to recognize and take ownership of the problem they had caused. Every problem has an owner. Failing to recognize your role in the issue can lead to a life of victimhood, where life is always happening to you and it's never your fault.

Sometimes it's the parents who need to admit they blew it. I think that has been a big key to staying connected with our kids. There have been so many times that we, as Mom and Dad, have had to say sorry for not protecting their hearts. We aren't perfect. We yell. We get frustrated. We lose our temper. We say harsh words. In our house we've created an atmosphere of freedom where our kids feel free to come to us and tell us if we've hurt their hearts. Not in a disrespectful or rude way. They want to keep connected to us just as much as we do to them. And, if we've said or done something to hurt them, then we have a responsibility to clean up whatever mess we've made in the relationship. I saw a quote recently that sums it up for us. "Cleaning up your mess with your kids doesn't teach failure. It teaches leadership." Our kids watch our every move. It's important that we show them how to clean up when messes are made and someone gets hurt.

Owning the Problem

I can't stress enough how important it is for kids to learn to take ownership of their actions. Playing the blame game isn't going to get them far in life and perpetuates a victim mentality. Creating a safe space to fail and then clean up the messes that failure may have caused is vital to a healthy outlook on life. Mike and I did this by working very hard on leading by example. Countless times I personally have had to take ownership of my actions and towards my kids. I've had to apologize multiple times for flying off the handle or speaking in an unkind tone.

In December 2012, all four of my kids got the flu. They were ages twelve, ten, eight, and five. It started with one and when I took them to the doctor, he informed me that all my kids would have it by the time it was through the house. He was correct. One by one they fell sick. Every couple of days another would come to me running a fever. I ended up setting up mattresses in the living room so I could attend to them more easily. We had our own little Talley sick bay. For two weeks I was on nursing duty and was steadily becoming more and more exhausted. As well as more and more disappointed because we had had to cancel one Christmas tradition after another. No sugar cookie decorating, no piling into the car and getting hot cocoa to see the Christmas lights, and no Christmas crafts. The only thing we had time to do was possibly decorating gingerbread houses, so I had Mike stop at the store and grab some so we could salvage Christmas. I was so excited. I hadn't been out of the house in weeks and was over all the sickness. I told the kids and all of them had zero interest in decorating houses. I was devastated. I yelled at them all and told them they were ungrateful and didn't care about Christmas and that I was just trying to bring some joy into the house. My parting remarks were, "I'm putting myself in time out!" and I slammed my bedroom door leaving four flu-ridden children and a tired daddy behind me. Not a proud moment for me. There is nothing more humbling than having to tell your sick children you are sorry for yelling at them. They all forgave me and I think we ended up doing the houses a couple of days later. It was a Christmas they would forever refer to as "the Christmas that Mom had a meltdown."

I've had to go back, sometimes hours later, and clean up a mess I've made with all my kids. One at a time, taking them aside to make sure their hearts are OK. Mike has had to do the same thing. We humbled ourselves enough to say, "I screwed up big time. Will you please forgive me?" From the time they were small to their last week as teenagers, Mike and I have always worked to own our part in a problem. We lead by example, realizing that we couldn't ask something of them that we weren't able to manage ourselves.

One of the ways we helped them in taking ownership of their problems is never making our kids feel like they had to lie to us. We combatted this by giving them permission to tell the truth without a hammer coming down on their head. If they came to us and confessed an issue or something they did wrong, we always embraced them and told them we were proud of them for coming to us. We would work through the issue, but never got angry or punished them for being brave. We would make a big deal out of them taking ownership and telling the truth. The rule of the house was if you are honest, even if it's hard, then there wouldn't be punishment, but we would come alongside them to help them through the issue. I think that coupled with giving them space to mess up, helped curb them feeling afraid to come to us with anything. It wasn't that lying was eliminated from the house. My kids are like any others, and we had our moments over the years of having to address that issue, but I can only remember a handful of times that it was a problem.

Forgiveness

Our approach to forgiveness is simple, honestly. Jesus tells us to forgive each other so our heavenly Father will forgive us. When asked how many times we should forgive someone who sins against us, he told us to forgive over and over until forever. We started with just the obedience part of it.

> "If you forgive those who sin against you, your heavenly Father will forgive you. But if you refuse to forgive others, your Father will not forgive your sins." (Matthew 6:14–15, NLT)

Jesus said do it, so we do. This verse is on my list of top ten scary verses in the Bible. We have to forgive, or we won't be forgiven. Telling someone I forgive you doesn't condone what happened. We teach our children that forgiveness is releasing the other person to the Lord and sometimes we must forgive multiple times because we can choose to pick up our hurt and offense over and over.

We teach them that holding on to unforgiveness makes us bitter and unable to connect well with others. So, even if they don't feel it yet, saying those words releases them from that burden.

> Then Peter came to him and asked, "Lord, how often should I forgive someone who sins against me? Seven times?"
>
> "No not seven times," Jesus replied, "but seventy times seven." (Matthew 18:21–22, NLT)

Some people argue that they need to see repentance first, but I honestly don't see that in the Bible anywhere. If your brother is sinning against you over and over, there is a definite lack of heart change, but Jesus doesn't tell us to forgive seventy times seven only if your brother has repented. No, he tells us to forgive regardless. Our hearts will catch up and God will honor the obedience. I guess you could say we practiced forgiveness until it became second nature. They learned to forgive quickly by practicing it.

Repentance
The end goal of cleaning up messes we've made is always repentance in the end. True repentance will bear fruit of a change of heart and behavior. It will bring about the fruit of the Spirit as a matter of fact.

> "But the Holy Spirit produces this kind of fruit in our lives: love, joy, peace, patience, kindness, goodness, faithfulness, gentleness, and self-control. There is no law against these things!" (Galatians 5:22–23, NLT)

We have learned that repentance sometimes takes time. There are times that we are sometimes dealing with the same issue over and over either with ourselves or our children. These are times that we extend grace and forgiveness many times over. There is sometimes a process or refinement taking place that isn't instantaneous. We tell our children that everybody has issues or things they are working on. The main point being that we are working on our problems. When we see even the slightest difference in behavior then we make a big deal about it. I call it "praising the mundane." It may seem insignificant to others, but any small amount of heart change takes an enormous amount of self-control. It helps to know that our hard work is seen. It may only be a slight turn in the right direction, but it's always celebrated because working on your problems is hard. It's super hard for adults and five times as hard for children to, one, own the problem and, two, work to change the problem.

Repent means to turn around. We like to think of it as doing it differently. Whatever it may be, in order to make that change, we have to do it differently next time. Mike tells the kids, "Choose to do it differently this time." There is always a "more excellent" way of doing life. If we have an anger problem, then we work on not reacting. If we have a disrespect problem, then we work on the words and tone of our speech. If we have a disobedience problem, we work on obeying even when it's hard. If we have a complaining problem, then we work on viewing the world through eyes of thankfulness.

A Place at the Table
Letting our children have a voice has been probably one of my favorite parts of the way we parented. We decided at some point that we would give our children permission to confront us in love. Just beware that if you decide to do this, your children will humble you faster than you can blink. Remembering that honor is one of our core values, it helped us to know the

kids were understanding it when they recognized dishonor and called it out. One story I can remember was an interaction that happened between Charles and Mike when Charles was around ten years old. Mike mentioned this story in an earlier chapter. They were driving in a car and Mike was fussing at Charles for something. His tone was less than gentle and his voice was rising. Charles very calmly and quietly said, "Dad, you don't have to be so harsh."

Mike said those words went straight to his heart. Mike told him he was right. "There was no reason for Dad to be so harsh" and he went on explaining his thoughts more gently. Charles recognized Mike's tone as dishonor. He knew that it wasn't the way we were supposed to handle things, and he spoke up when he saw it happening. So many times we feel that the correction or feedback only has to go one way, but is that really relationship? Is it possible to open the dialogue a bit so our kids can recognize and speak to the things they see as wrong, even if it's us? Can we humble ourselves enough as parents to receive the feedback our children have to give us? Countless times my children have come to me and told me I hurt them with my tone or words as I have with them. It's become a way of life in our house.

We've all heard the expression, "Children should be seen and not heard," and I've always felt that statement was a bit unfair. Children have thoughts and feelings, and I know I've gleaned a lot of wisdom from things that have come out of my children's mouths. I realize that there is a correct way for them to speak up and, of course, there are times when speaking up may not be appropriate, but that comes with training, maturity, and allowing them to make mistakes along the way. I can always have a conversation and redirect them later. Kids have amazing things to say. The more we let them express themselves the better they will get at it. It's OK for them to have their own thoughts and opinions within our relationship.

I love how Jesus modeled how to view children for us. He honored the children around him. When the disciples were pushing them aside, Jesus was gathering them close and defending them. He was giving them a "place at the table." He knew there was so much in their hearts. Just the amount of faith they have is incredible. He wanted them close to him so they could be given the attention they so deserved. I can just imagine him listening intently to every word. Giving our children a place at the table makes them feel seen and heard. It opens the door for honest conversations and heart connections. We, as parents, are communicating to them that their feelings and opinions are valid and deserve to be heard. We don't always agree with them and there have been tough conversations as we seek to understand their hearts, but that shadows in comparison to the fruit we have seen by just taking time to simply listen to understand.

• CHAPTER 10 •

Sometimes We Serve—Mike Talley

"I wish I were a kitten so I could have a baby now and not wait till I was married."
—Madilyn (age 6)

GROWING UP, MY PARENTS taught me how to serve others. I didn't understand it at the time that they were teaching me a core value. A core value that has had a huge impact on my life and on how we have raised our family. When I was younger, there were a few times my dad took me along to help mow someone's yard. We didn't get paid for it and when I asked him, he simply said, "She doesn't have a lot of money and her yard needed mowing."

The church I grew up in rented a space that we only used on Sundays. Like many small churches of that time, we had metal folding chairs. My dad would often volunteer to set up the chairs Saturday night for the Sunday service. When it was his turn, he would take me. It was hard work and I know I complained, but he would just tell me it was good for me and built character. Sunday after church, the pastor would dismiss the congregation and it was expected that all the boys and young men would help put up all the chairs. To this day, when I see metal folding chairs, I am reminded of all the times I had to set them up or put them away. So many smashed fingers when they would slip. Then, there were endless churchwork days, church rummage sales, and helping people move. Being a part of a small church gave you lots of opportunities to serve.

When I was thirteen, I joined the Boy Scouts. This gave all sorts of new opportunities to serve. After all, the Boy Scout slogan is "Do a good turn daily." We helped clean up vacant lots, picked up trash, and helped other scouts with their service projects.

Somewhere along the way, I discovered that serving others brought me tremendous joy and satisfaction. This did not happen by accident. It only happened because I was taught how to serve and the importance of serving others. The funny thing is, when we started having our own children, teaching them how to serve others wasn't really in our minds. We just kept doing the things our parents had taught us. When the kids were a bit older, we noticed that a fair number of their friend group lived lives that seemed largely divorced from our core value of serving. It was at that point that it finally clicked: You must teach serving and the best way to do that is for parents to model a servant's heart to their children.

Jesus is our example. He is the perfect servant leader. The topic of servant leadership has had hundreds of books written about it and countless business seminars. It seems that any

Christian-based business will, at some point or another, teach their staff the concept of servant leadership. Some may say this is a fad, but Jesus' example is one that we should strive to emulate in our life and to teach to our children.

Jesus was fully man and fully God. Stepping down from heaven and becoming a man was a huge act of humility. Throughout his earthly ministry, Jesus showed that he was always willing to serve those in need. It did not matter their status—centurion (Matthew 8:5–13), synagogue leader and the woman with the issue of blood (Luke 8:40–56), the woman caught in adultery (John 8:3–11), lepers, the lame, the demon possessed—Jesus took time to serve each, so that each could have their need met. Jesus consistently modeled how to be a servant leader. He never lost sight of who he was, the Son of God, but his status as the Son of God was not diminished by his servanthood. This was in direct contrast to the world at that time and indeed even today. Even though Jesus was the perfect model, his disciples still did not understand. In Matthew 20, we see that James and John's mother came to ask Jesus for her sons to sit at the place of honor in heaven. James and John were still thinking of ruling over people. In their mind, that was what a leader did, a leader rules over people. A leader is shown honor and people should serve the leader. This was the complete opposite of the lifestyle Jesus modeled. It was revolutionary to them that you could be a leader AND serve. Jesus says in Matthew 20:28, "Just as the Son of Man did not come to be served, but to serve, and to give his life as a ransom for many."

The night Jesus was betrayed, he undertook one of the most menial acts of service: He washed his disciples' feet. This clearly made the disciples uneasy. After all this was the Messiah! The King! How could he be washing MY feet!

> 12 When he had finished washing their feet, he put on his clothes and returned to his place. "Do you understand what I have done for you?" he asked them. 13 **"You call me 'Teacher' and 'Lord,' and rightly so, for that is what I am. 14 Now that I, your Lord and Teacher, have washed your feet, you also should wash one another's feet. 15 I have set you an example that you should do as I have done for you.** 16 Very truly I tell you, no servant is greater than his master, nor is a messenger greater than the one who sent him. 17 Now that you know these things, you will be blessed if you do them. (John 13:12–17, NIV)

The question probably on your mind is: How do I model serving to my children?

The answer is simple, yet difficult at times: You teach by example.

When our kids were very young (the oldest was eight), we started helping lead a small church here in town. This was not a full-time ministry position; I still was working forty-plus hours a week at my engineering job. But being on the leadership team presented us with a ton of serving opportunities. Jen and I decided that where practical, where we went, the kids went with us. We took the position that instead of telling our kids how to serve, or simply modeling service to them, we would draw them in and have them serve alongside of us.

Our small church facility needed to be cleaned weekly. As a small start-up church, there was no room in the budget to hire a cleaning service, so we volunteered. Each week Jen would head up with all four kids in tow to clean the church. Each kid was given a task that was age-appropriate and they all pitched in to get the place clean. This was an opportunity to show the kids what serving looked like and, more importantly, we were able to explain the why.

If you have been around children any length of time, you will quickly learn that "Why?" is one of their favorite questions to ask. It's constant, day in and day out! Why? Why? Why? Their little minds sponging up all the information they can. I have found that if you take time to explain to your children what you are about to do and the why behind it, then it draws them in and helps them feel part of the process. Instead of telling the kids we are cleaning the church because we have to and because we are telling them to, we stopped to explain that, "We GET to serve the church. That this is a tremendous honor that the church trusts us enough to keep the building clean. And, guess what? You guys get to help us with this!" Then, we would explain that Jesus calls us to serve one another and that we should serve others as if we are severing Jesus himself. It wasn't like we had to explain this every time we headed up to the building to clean, but it was explained up front the first time and would be repeated as needed to those that lost focus as to why they were doing all this work.

My kids got to see that Mom and Dad were serving the church and that they got to help. Each time they finished cleaning the building, we would praise them for their servant's heart and tell them how proud we were of them.

Just as in my day, there was always an abundance of churchwork days. I have always loved working outdoors, so I always volunteered for the outdoor work. Whichever kid wanted to work with me outside would join me, while the others helped Jen work on the inside of the building. The building we were using at the time was surrounded by tall pine trees. The building roof had a gutter system that was always getting clogged with pine needles and pine cones. As one of the "younger" men in the church, I usually volunteered to get up on the roof and clean the gutters. The kids always wanted to join me, but it was too dangerous. But they kept asking. When Nate was around thirteen, I felt he was old enough to help on the roof. Much to his mother's worry, he scrambled up the ladder and I began to show him how to clean the gutters. It was a hot South Georgia Saturday and being on the roof was about like being on the surface of the sun, but Nate was proud. He was proud he was finally old enough to help the "men on the roof." He didn't even realize he was serving. I had brought him alongside and explained why we were working at the church, then I gave him various age-appropriate tasks to accomplish, finally, I explained that when he was older, he could help me on the roof. I'm exaggerating a bit to say this was a rite-of-passage moment, but in many ways it was.

Around that same time period (2014), I started a lawn care company to earn some extra money. The Lord had blessed me with a good job, but with only my income and four growing kids, we needed a little extra income. I would cut several nights after work and then all day of Saturday. I hired Nate as my worker and paid him $5 for each yard we did. His job was to pick up the pine cones and sticks and to run the edger for the walkway, driveway, and curbline, while I ran the big zero-turn mower. It was hot work. There were many Saturdays in July and August where we would do seven or more yards in one day. Not bad for a fourteen-year-old and a forty-one-year-old! All the while, Nate would earn $5 a yard. His younger brother, Charles (twelve at the time), was jealous of the money Nate was earning. I told him that his time would come.

The church building was located on a large lot. Prices from the local yard companies were way too high for the church to pay, so I volunteered to cut the yard for free. There were times when the church could afford to pay me, but at least 50% or more of the time, we did it for free. On the weeks we were doing it for free, I would tell Nate: "Hey, this week is a free week for the church, so you won't get paid your $5 for this yard. But we get to serve the church and take care of a need they have." At first Nate would grumble a bit, but after a while when we pulled up to the church lot he would ask, "Are we doing this one for free?" I would nod yes and he would hop out the door and get on his tasks.

A few years later, Nate "retired" from the lawn business and started working at the local Chick-fil-A. It was time to call

Charles up from the bench!

You need to understand that Charles is VERY MUCH an inside kid. He loves video games and to NOT be outside. But it was interesting to see how excited he was to be earning money with Dad. He had seen Nate for the last three cutting seasons leave out with Dad each Saturday and many weekday nights. He heard the tales of all the trouble Nate and I got into, such as wasps, stuck mower, broken mower, and crazy customers. He wanted to be a part of the team. Well, this was his chance. Just like Nate, I paid him $5 a yard. And just like Nate, I explained to him about how we get to serve the church and how sometimes we don't get paid for the work. He understood and didn't miss a beat.

A year or so into Charles' tenure, one of my customers fell and broke a few bones. She is an older single lady who was a substitute teacher but did not always have steady income. I knew that she would not be able to work for a good bit of time and that her budget was surely going to suffer. I talked to Charles about it and told him I felt that the Lord wanted us to cut her yard for free until she got back on her feet. It blessed me that he agreed and understood, even though it meant he would not be getting his $5 for her yard.

Volunteering at church brought all sorts of serving opportunities. Our church moved to our downtown and started handing out coffee at city events. These events were almost always outside events: Christmas parade, street festivals, etc. By this time, the kids were older and so Jen and I would divide and conquer. Oftentimes, this meant that one of us would go in the morning with a few kids to help set up and serve for a bit at the event and then the other would come later in the day to finish the event and clean up. We would give the kids choices on which part they wanted to help with. By now, serving had become such second nature to them that it wasn't a question of if they would help, but of where they would help.

We did so many events where it was sweltering hot or very cold, yet the kids always served alongside Jen and I. The other members of the church would always compliment the kids and tell them they were doing a great job. Many of our members had "adopted" our kids as their own or as their grandkids, and it brought them such joy to see young people serving the Lord.

These are just a few examples of how we modeled servanthood to our kids and how we had them walk alongside us to be part of the process.

You may be reading this realizing that you have never cultivated a culture of serving in your family. You may have already raised your family or are just about to start your family. What can you do? The good news is that it isn't too late. Sure, it's easier if you start when your children are young, as it becomes part of their life, but you can always start now. How? You jump in and model it for them and bring them in close, alongside you. If you have already raised your family, then take time with your grandkids. Teach them. If you are just starting out, find older parents and ask them how they taught their kids.

Below are some helpful tips:

- Model serving yourself. This is the only way to teach proper servanthood. Your kids need to see that you believe in what you are doing.
- Serve alongside your children. Kids need to buy in and the easiest way to get their buy in is to get them working with you, so they feel like they are part of the process.
- Praise your kids when they serve. Even if you had to pull them kicking and screaming, when you are done, tell them what a great job they did.
- Explain the why. Instead of "because I said so," take the time to explain the why of your service to your church, city, organization, or others.

Final Thoughts

CHILDREN ARE A GIFT from the Lord. He has given them to us to parent and steward for such a short time in the scheme of things. The precious gift of parenting isn't something to be taken lightly. They are only in our care for a few short years before they start their own journey in parenting, so there is a sense of responsibility to love and cherish this time we have with them.

The heart of this book has been to shine a light on parenting from the perspective of connection and relationship. Without either of these taking precedent, we end up parenting from a place of fear and control and this is not the heart of our heavenly Father. Parenting from a place of connection first produces love, gentleness, and kindness that foster trust between parents and children.

Sometimes We Wear Pajamas to Church is not a self-help book. It is a book about what has worked for us in our parenting journey. I hope everyone who reads it comes away with a fresh revelation of how the Father loves and how we can model that for our children. Parenting is not for the faint of heart. As you just read, the learning curve for Mike and I has been massive. The main things I think I would tell a parent in front of me is to choose connection first, model the attributes you want to see from your children, clean up parenting messes quickly, get your healing so you don't parent out of your pain, and extend grace to your children and yourself.

To lift a quote from the beginning of this book:

"Parenting has been the most fun, aggravating, terrifying, and satisfying season of our lives. The responsibility is overwhelming sometimes, yet the joy of it all brings us to tears. This is our journey of learning to love our children the way God loves us and doing our best to lead them with gentleness and kindness."

Recommended Readings:

Loving Our Kids on Purpose: Making a Heart-to-Heart Connection
Danny Silk

Love and Logic Magic for Early Childhood: Practical parenting from Birth to Six Year
Jim Fay and Charles Fay, Ph.D.

Directing Vision Daily: Biblical Parenting (DVD series)
Danny Silk

Beyond Consequences, Logic, and Control: A Love-Based Approach to Helping Attachment-Challenged Children with Severe Behaviors
Heather T. Forbes, LCSW and B. Bryan Post

The Connected Child: Bring Hope and Healing to Your Adoptive Family
Karyn B. Purvis, Ph.D., David R. Cross, Ph.D., and Wendy Lyons Sunshine

The Body Keeps Score: Brain, Mind and Body in the Healing of Trauma
Bessel Van Der Kolk, M.D.
Raising Spirit Led Kids: Guiding Kids to Walk Naturally in the Supernatural
Seth Dahl

Designing God's Dream Home: Secrets to Experiencing Stress-Free Cooperation From Your Kids (Without Anger or Feeling Guilty) As You Discover God's Blueprint For Your Family
Seth Dahl

Brave Communication (DVD series)
Dann Farrelly

www.ingramcontent.com/pod-product-compliance
Lightning Source LLC
LaVergne TN
LVHW011206080426
835508LV00007B/622